PENTECOSTALISM IN
THE CHURCH

PENTECOSTALISM IN THE CHURCH

By JAMES D. BALES

Copyright 1972
By Lambert Book House

Published By
LAMBERT BOOK HOUSE
Box 4007
Shreveport, Louisiana 71104

DEDICATION
TO
J. PORTER WILHITE
*Valiant Soldier of
Christ and the Cross
Who has preached for over Sixty Years*

TABLE OF CONTENTS

Chapters   *Page*

INTRODUCTION 3

I. BIBLICAL MIRACLES 7

II. SOME CHARACTERISTICS OF THE MOVEMENT 25

III. FALSE DOCTRINES AND CONTRADICTIONS .. 39

IV. THE SUFFICIENCY OF SCRIPTURES 49

V. THE GIFTS HAVE CEASED 57

VI. WHAT SHALL WE DO? 61

VII. A REVIEW OF "THEY SPEAK WITH OTHER TONGUES" 66
    Lay Aside Logic 66
    The Leap of Faith 69
    Did He See the Lord? 73
    The Tumbling Walls 79
    Seeking the Baptism of the Spirit 83
    Evidences of Baptism in the Spirit? 88
    Witnesses and Power 92
    Sherrill and Tongues 96
    They Speak With Other Tongues? 100
    Religion Without Joy 106
    Resisting the Spirit? 110

Introduction

What has been known historically as Pentecostalism is called the "new Pentecostalism" in an article which was reprinted in *Logos,* an international journal of the charismatic movement. (Jan.-Feb., 1972, p. 26) Pentecostalism emphasizes the Holy Spirit in miraculous manifestations such as tongues and healing. Historically it has been known as Pentecostalism, and since this term is a broader term than "the tongues movement", we shall use the word Pentecostalism to refer to the position that the miraculous gifts are for Christians today.

Pentecostalism has penetrated almost every religious body today and some denominationalists have called it the third force in Christendom. The other two forces are viewed as Catholicism and Protestantism.

Pat Boone, whose ideas I discussed in *Pat Boone and the Gift of Tongues,* is the most prominent leader in this movement among us. Over 400,000 copies of his book, *A New Song,* have been published. It is now available in a paperback edition. Shirley Boone has written a book on a woman liberated.

I am convinced that Pentecostalism is but a new trial of old errors. In some of its features, such as extreme emotionalism and ecstatic utterances, it is a revival of some errors which were found in paganism before Christ came to this earth. R. A. Knox deals with different groups which, over the centuries, have claimed inspiration, tongues, and other assumed miraculous manifestations. He concentrates on movements from around 1660 to 1750, and includes early Methodist. (*Enthusiasm,* Oxford: At the Clarendon Press, 1962 Reprint)

The zeal of some Pentecostals puts to shame some members of the church, although there are those who are as zealous, or more so, without partaking of their errors. Zeal is important, but it should be according to knowledge. (Rom. 10:1-4) Some who are "turned on" for a period of time are later "turned off".

In our evaluation of Pentecostalism we are not trying to weaken anyone's faith in Christ but to enlighten their faith. Just because some have left drugs and other forms of immorality and self-destruction for Pentecostalism does not mean that we ought not to evaluate its teaching in the light of the Bible. The author would much prefer that they be in Pentecostalism than in the immorality in which some of them were involved. However, even good people need to be instructed more perfectly in the way of the Lord; including instruction concerning baptism into Christ. (Acts 18:24-19:7) One is not trying to weaken faith by asking people to examine their own doctrines in the light of the Bible. We need to be sure that we are depending on what God has promised (Rom. 4:20-21), and not on what men have promised us or we have promised ourselves.

It is possible to be wrong both in diagnosis and in prescription, but it is possible also to be right in diagnosis and wrong in prescription. Because there are some things wrong with Christians today, as there were also in the first century, does not mean that the cure is to seek the baptism of the Spirit and the miraculous gifts.

A PROBLEM IN THE CHURCH?

The threat of Pentecostalism to the church has been headed off as a major movement, in the author's judgment, because some were alert to its presence and dealt with it before it "swarmed". However, it had made some inroads and the threat is not over yet. Pat Boone is one evidence of its presence. A booklet has been published which tells of the conversion of some preachers and others. It is *The Acts of the Holy Spirit in the Church of Christ Today.* Another evidence of its presence is found in the fact that Bob Miller, of the Board of Directors of Youth Outreach Foundation, Inc., refused to answer my question — both when I phoned him and when I wrote him — whether or not he believed he had the gift of "tongues" as does Pat. Outreach Tours is a division of the Foundation, and their literature said: "Our Board of Directors includes Pat Boone, George Otis and Bob Miller." George Otis is one who helped convert Pat Boone and, as far as I can find out, has never claimed to be a member of the church of Christ.

I have learned of cells of tongues speakers in congregations in different parts of the country and in some colleges maintained by the brethren. In at least one case, a missionary has been carried away into the movement.

WHY?

What are some of the reasons why Pentecostalism has made

INTRODUCTION 5

some inroads into the church? *First,* the mistaken view that miraculous gifts are an essential and permanent part of Christianity. We have had — in the main — an untaught generation on the nature, characteristics, purposes, and duration of the gifts. It takes only one generation to have an untaught generation. *Second,* its popularity in the religious world leads some to seek the gifts. *Third,* the cold formalism of some contributed to a reaction into emotionalism on the part of others. Some have lived starved emotional lives, they do not have an understanding of their own emotions, and they have been swept off their feet by something which brought more "life" and excitement into their religion. *Fourth,* some become tired of what they have believed and want something new. *Fifth,* some have itching ears, do not love the truth, and receive strong delusions. (2 Thess. 2:10-12; 2 Tim. 4:3-4) *Sixth,* all of us are inadequate, and some have thought that their inadequacies, or some of them, have been overcome by the gifts. *Seventh,* a congenial atmosphere has been prepared by the philosophies of existentialism which are taught in much of the literature, arts, etc., today. Existentialism has stressed the freedom of man from external authority, the importance of doing "one's own thing," the emotions have been emphasized, and personal experience has been proclaimed as the authority for religion and morality. Attitudes similar to these are found in Pentecostalism as it exists among us. Religion to them is a personal thing in the sense that one does his own thing and finds satisfaction in it even if it does not conform to the Bible. Emotional experiences are often sought after and are viewed as a divine confirmation of the truth of their teaching concerning baptism of the Holy Spirit, and often on many other subjects. *Eighth,* some maintain that if one accepts the finality of the written revelation in the Bible, that he has but a dead letter; or a word with little power. In order to have power, and for the word to be really authoritative in our life, one must have the word made alive by miraculous gifts. There are many of them who go on to feel that they are free from the need to conform strictly to the teaching of the Bible. *Ninth,* the way has also been prepared by the fact that there are some people who have become so broad in their fellowship that they refuse to draw the line against *advocates* of the gifts. In some cases they may say that they do not have the gifts, but "who are they to say that these people do not"? They may say that they think these people are mistaken but they should have the freedom to teach in our midst, without being disfellowshipped. There are others who shrink from contending for the faith (Jude 3), but they contend against those who oppose the inroads of the tongues movement.

While we should not conduct the defense of the faith in the spirit of the world, we must be set for the defense of the gospel. (Phil. 1:7, 16) Although some may tire of controversy, and none of us should live in the "objective case and the kickative mood", we cannot be faithful without contending for the faith in the spirit of love for God, for truth, for those who are being led astray, and for those who are leading them astray. We may somtimes tire of the warfare in which the Christian life involves us on so many fronts, but as good soldiers of the cross we must continue to fight the good fight of faith.

Although we should be patient, and study long with those who are having problems in this or other matters, it is quite another thing if the individual is a problem in that he is creating cells of tongues speakers and advocating it in this and other ways.

We shall not be able to cover in depth the subject of Pentecostalism in the church in this brief book. The interested reader is referred to our fuller discussions in *Pat Boone and the Gift of Tongues, Miracles or Mirages?*, and *The Holy Spirit and the Christian*. There is some material in this discussion which is not included in these books. Jimmy Jividen has a recent book on *Glossolalia, From God or Man?* (Fort Worth, Texas: Star Bible Publications, 1971)

Chapter I

Biblical Miracles

Because the natural and the supernatural are both from God, some people do not distinguish between the miraculous and the natural. However, if anyone knows the difference between how Adam's wife arrived in the world, and how his own wife arrived, he knows the difference between the miraculous and the nonmiraculous. He who can distinguish between growing grapes and making wine, and immediately turning water into wine, can know the difference between a supernatural action, which is a sign, and the natural which is not a sign. (John 2:11)

Miracles were involved in the revelation and confirmation of the word of God, the seed of the kingdom. (1 Cor. 2:10-14; Heb. 2:3-4; Lk. 8:11) But the new birth is not a miracle because it is brought about by the Spirit through the word of God, the seed of the kingdom. Spiritual laws, not supernatural manifestations, operate in and bring about the new birth. When God so willed, He worked a miracle whether the person on whom it was worked wanted it done or not. Saul had not asked for the supernatural appearance of Christ. (Acts 9:1, 3-6, 17) Elymas did not want to be struck blind. (Acts 13:7-12) However, the new birth — even in the case of Saul — could not take place against the will of the individual. One must believe and be willing to submit to God's word in order to undergo the new birth.

MIRACLES DEFINED

What the Bible means by "miracle" can be determined by the words used to describe miracles, and what is said of miracles. They were "mighty works and wonders and signs." (Acts 2:22) As miracles (mighty works, or powers), they pointed "to the divine power which is operative in the event or act, the invisible, supernatural source of energy which makes the phenomenon possible." Miracles were wonders because they led to amazement and astonishment on the part of the beholders. As signs they signified the presence of one endowed with supernatural power. They constituted one, but only one, of the certifications that the worker was sent of God and had a message from God. They were to confirm the word. (Matt. 11:4-5; Mk. 16:20; Acts 14:3; Heb. 2:4) As Vernon C. Grounds puts it: "Synthesizing the root connotations of these terms, we may define a miracle biblically as an observable phenomenon effected by the direct operation of God's power, an arresting deviation from the ordinary sequences of nature, a deviation calculated to elicit faith-begetting awe, a divine inbreaking which authenticates a revelational agent." (Everett F. Harrison, Editor-in-chief, *Baker's Dictionary of Theology,* Grand Rapids, Michigan: Baker Book House, 1960, p. 365)

The mighty miracles Moses wrought in Egypt were signs and wonders. (Deut. 34:10-12) When Moses and the magicians got into a contest, before it was over, Pharaoh knew who was on God's side.

It needs to be stressed that miracles were signs to confirm the word of the miracle worker. It showed that his message was from God. Jesus promised the "sign of Jonah". (Matt. 16:4) God approved Jesus by miracles (Acts 2:22), Mark briefly stated the purpose of the miracles as that of "confirming the word by the signs that followed". (Mk. 16:20; Acts 10:44-47; 11:1, 17-18; 15:7-8, 12) Therefore, we are told that the Lord bore *"witness unto the word* of his grace, granting signs and wonders to be done *by their hands."* (Acts 14:3) The tongues themselves were signs to confirm the word. (Mk. 16:17, 20; Acts 2:4, 6, 8, 11, 33; 1 Cor. 14:5-6, 27-28, 22) Paul, as the apostle to the Gentiles, had special need for the gift of tongues since he confronted so many people who had their own different native speech. (Acts 14:11; 22:21; 26:17; Rom. 15:16-20, 28; Gal. 2:8-9) Therefore, we do not wonder that he spoke in tongues more than anyone in Corinth. (1 Cor. 14:18)

It is often true that sincere Pentecostals are deceived in thinking that some people have received the Spirit when these people themselves realized then or later that they had not received the Spirit. *First,* some people realize that they simply became worked up emotionally and imitated others. *Second,* a student told me years ago that he attended services of a Pentecostal church but could not get the "Spirit". Finally, he decided that he would get the "Spirit" during a certain meeting. Sometimes they tell an individual to claim it and he will receive it. This is similar to telling them to start talking in non-English sounds and the Spirit will take over and they will speak in tongues. So this person decided to claim the Spirit in faith in order to get the baptism of the Spirit. He went to the altar and carried on as the others were carrying on. A number of the sisters said that he had it. He told me he did not have anything. He left the building and never went back. Why could some of them not discern that he did not have the Spirit? *Third,* another student said he was the only one of the young people who had not received the Spirit in a revival meeting. "At a prayer meeting at our house one night, it was decided

BIBLICAL MIRACLES 9

that I should receive the Spirit so all began praying. I remember that it was very hot, fans were buzzing, and I went to sleep repeating, 'Thank you, Jesus'. I said it so long it wasn't coming out clear — someone said '. . . has it.' " However, he did not have anything. *Fourth,* one person came into a service and heard "one or two words of his friend's speech in tongues. He interpreted them for at least thirty minutes."

There are so many cases which show how easily many of these people are deceived into thinking someone has the Spirit in a miraculous way, when in reality he does not have anything miraculous and has not received the Spirit in a special sense. How could this be true if their position is right? Are there no discerners of spirits, or teachers, among them?

IF ANY, ALL

If any of the miraculous gifts are available today, all are available. There is no ground on which to say that some are for us today, but the others have ceased. Not everyone would have all the gifts, but all of them should be manifested in their movement. What miraculous gifts were given in the first century? *First,* James exhorted all Christians to pray for wisdom — which has to do with the right use of knowledge and is not a prayer for a revelation of knowledge. (Jas. 1:5) God does not work a miracle in answering this prayer any more than He works a miracle, and feeds us with manna, in answering our prayer for daily bread. (Matt. 6:11; John 6:31-32) The gift of wisdom of which Paul spoke was a supernatural word of wisdom, for all did not have it. (1 Cor. 12:8-11, 29-30) Insofar as my experience goes, Pentecostals do not manifest more wisdom than people who do not claim the gifts. In fact, some of them often act very unwisely.

Second, the word of knowledge whereby truth was revealed by inspiration. (1 Cor. 12:8; 2:12-13)

Third, the gift of faith. This was not the ordinary faith which comes by hearing God's word, for all Christians have this faith. (Rom. 10:17) Not everyone had the gift of faith. (1 Cor. 12:9) Paul does not explain what it is, but it was a faith which was involved in working miracles. (1 Cor. 13:2; compare Jas. 5:15)

Fourth, gifts of healing. (1 Cor. 12:9)

Fifth, the working of miracles. (1 Cor. 12:10) This must have included more than the healing miracles; which Paul had just mentioned.

Sixth, the gift of prophecy which could involve prediction but was by no means limited to it. It included consolation, exhortation, and edification in that men were taught God's will. (1 Cor. 14:3-4, 24-25, 29-30)

Seventh, the discerning of spirits. (1 Cor. 12:10) Why is it that there are some leaders among them who have deceived them but none of them discerned it? We discern them by measuring them by God's will. (1 John 4:1-2; 1 Cor. 14:37)

Eighth, the tongues were languages. (1 Cor. 12:10; Acts 2:4, 6, 8, 11) But Pentecostals have to learn the language of the people to whom they preach. There are multitudes of them who maintain that tongues are ecstatic utterances, but this contradicts the Bible for the tongues promised in Mk. 16:17-18, 20, and which began to be fulfilled on Pentecost (Acts 2:4, 6, 8, 11), were languages spoken by men. If the Pentecostals had miraculous gifts of the Spirit, they would know that tongues were languages and not ecstatic utterances. Their ignorance discredits their claims. Furthermore, they would know that tongues were for a sign for unbelievers, and not designed as a sign to believers that they had been baptized in the Spirit. (Mk. 16:17-18, 20; 1 Cor. 14:22) Then, too, they would know that not everyone had the gift of tongues, and yet some of them claim that everyone should be baptized in the Spirit and speak in tongues. (1 Cor. 12:4-11, 30) In addition to this, they would realize that the tongues were not given to people as a private prayer language but as a public sign to convince unbelievers. (Mk. 16:17-18, 20; 1 Cor. 14:22) These things are sufficient to discredit their claims, for the Holy Spirit would not give them miraculous power to accredit teaching which contradicts the Spirit's teaching in the New Testament.

William J. Samarin has attended Pentecostal meetings in the United States, Canada, Italy, Jamaica and Holland over a period of five years. He wrote: "I have interviewed glossolalists and I have tape-recorded and analyzed countless samples of tongues." ("Glossolalia," *Psychology Today,* August 1972, p. 49) Although he held these people in respect, he concluded: "In every case, *glossolalia* turns out to be linguistic nonsense. A person filled by the Holy Spirit does not speak a foreign human tongue, although glossolalists believe that it is the language of angels." (p. 49)

"The speaker controls the rhythm, volume, speed and inflection of his speech so that the sounds emerge as pseudolanguage — in the form of words and sentences . . . *glossolalia* is fundamentally not language." (p. 50)

"The speaker uses vowel and consonant sounds, repeating them with a few variations. Anyone can produce a phrase that will pass as *glossolalia* if he is willing to drop his inhibitions. The manufacture of nonsense is quite literally child's play." (p. 50)

"Indeed, glossolalia is closer to improvisational jazz than it is to language. One tongues-speaker made this comparison for me. The speaker uses syllables the way a musician uses notes. Glossolalic sounds have no fixed semantic meaning. Tongues-speakers cannot communicate specific ideas or facts, but they can use tongues as a vehicle to *express* themselves in the way music expresses emotional experience. This explains why some individuals claim to understand the message contained in a speaker's glossolalic 'prophecy.' They react to his tone of voice, to his breathing and to gestures rather than to the semantics of a language." (p. 50)

He met some claims that tongues were actually languages but on examination he found them to be false.

People sought tongues for such reasons as their belief that it was a proof that they were baptized in the Spirit, because it represented the giving up of self and manifested what they viewed as complete submission to God, and because they felt that they could not satisfactorily express their worship in ordinary praise.

(The article in *Psychology Today* was taken from Samarin's book *Tongues of Men and Angels,* published in 1972 by the Macmillan Co.)

Ninth, interpretation of tongues. (1 Cor. 12:10; 14:15, 27-28)

Tenth, prophets and other inspired teachers were mentioned by Paul, and were implied in the fact of the gift of prophecy. (1 Cor. 12:28; Eph. 4:11) Will people today affirm inspiration and authority for their writings as Paul did for his? (1 Cor. 14:37)

Eleventh, helps, the nature of which was not specified. (1 Cor. 12:28)

Twelfth, governments. (1 Cor. 12:28) We are not told who these "wise counsels" were but it may refer to those who had the gift of wisdom.

There was also the gift of apostleship, which we shall discuss in the next section. At this place we raise the question, why are so many of them zealous for tongues but not for some of these other gifts? Why do they claim that tongues are for all, but do not claim that each one of these gifts is for each and every faithful Christian? There is no ground on which to say that tongues are for all without saying that all of the gifts are for all.

It is so easy for them to be deceived into thinking they have the gift of tongues, once they are convinced that tongues are ecstatic utterances. For anyone, as some of them are instructed, can start out on his own uttering non-English sounds and then think that the Spirit takes over and enables him to speak in tongues.

The Gift of Apostleship

"God hath set some in the church, first apostles . . . are all apostles?" (1 Cor. 12:28-29) All were not apostles, but some were. They were such by gift, and not by man's will. "Wherefore he said, When he ascended on high, he led captivity captive, and gave gifts unto men. . . . And he gave some to be apostles. . . ." (Eph. 4:8, 11) The apostleship is discussed in 1 Cor. 12 along with the other gifts. Gifts were embodied in, and manifested through, men. Some of these men, such as the apostles, held positions of authority in the church. The apostles were the supreme authority on earth. (Acts 2:42)

The Mormons are far more consistent, in their error, than are most modern speakers in 'tongues.' The Mormons maintain that if we have any of these gifts today we should have all of these gifts, including apostles of Jesus Christ. Furthermore, since the apostles and the prophets wrote inspired Scripture, if we have such today they should write more scripture. If anyone speaks today by the direct inspiration of the Holy Spirit, instead of by learning and teaching what the Spirit revealed in the Bible, we have an inspired message from God. Where are the inspired apostles, and the authoritative and new scriptures? Those who claim the gift of tongues, or of any of the other gifts, should produce inspired scriptures in addition to the New Testament. However, they cannot do so, and the claims of those who give us such "scriptures" can be discredited on the basis of their lack of evidence and their contradicting the Bible.

QUALIFICATIONS OF APOSTLES

What were the qualifications of the apostles of Christ? Before considering these, we need to remember that the term apostle covers more than the apostles of Christ. The word itself meant one who was sent by another. Therefore, it is used of Christ, for God sent Him from heaven (Heb. 3:1), and of messengers, or those sent, by congregations on some special work. This included taking money from one place to another, or being sent to help someone in the work of the gospel. Epaphroditus was the messenger, or apostle, of the church in Philippi. (Phil. 2:25) Those appointed to help convey the contribution, which was for the relief of the poor among the saints in Jerusalem, were apostles or messengers of the churches. (2 Cor. 8:19, 23)

The apostles of Christ were a special group of messengers who were selected, qualified, and appointed by Christ. They were called to a unique work. Their work was a continuation of Christ's ministry and a witness to His resurrection. (John 15:16, 27; 17:6-8, 15, 20-21; Acts 1:8; 2:32) Therefore, they had special qualifications. First, theirs was a ministry of witnesses. They had witnessed the personal ministry of Christ, and had seen Him after His resurrection. (John 15:16, 27; Acts 1:8, 22; 2:32; 3:15; 4:20, 33; 5:32; 10:39; 1 John 1:1-4) As eye and ear witnesses to the works and resurrection of Christ, they cannot have successors. (Acts 1:21, 22; 10:39-42; 22:14-15; 23:11; 1 Cor. 9:1) Who today was with the Lord in His personal ministry? If we must have a repetition of the work of the apostles, why must we not also have a repetition in our generation of the personal ministry of Christ; of which their ministry was one of its direct results?

Second, the apostles were called and chosen by Christ personally. (Lk. 6:13; Acts 1:2; 9:6; 24:16-18; Gal. 1:1)

Third, the apostles learned a lot of the truth from Jesus personally. They taught these truths, as well as the rest of the truth, as they were directly inspired by the Holy Spirit. (John 14:26; 16:7-13) Paul was not taught by man, but by revelation of Jesus Christ. (Gal. 1:12)

Fourth, the apostles had authority not only in one congregation but in the universal church. Their commission was one of universal authority which was exercised in submission to the will of Christ, the only head of the church. (John 13:16, 20; 14:26; 16:12-15; Acts 2:42; 1 Cor. 4:17; 11:2, 23; 14:37; 2 Cor. 11:28; 10:13-16; 13:10; Rom. 1:14-16; 2 Thess. 2:15; 3:5-6, 12-15)

Fifth, they performed a wide variety of miracles to confirm the fact that they were apostles of Christ and their message was inspired. (Acts 2:43; 2 Cor. 12:12; Heb. 2:2-4; Acts 5:19; 12:6-9; 9:37-40; 3:2-8; 28:6) Paul spoke in tongues, worked miracles, cast out demons, etc. (Acts 19:11-12; 1 Cor. 14:18)

Sixth, they had the power to communicate miraculous gifts through the laying on of their hands. (Acts 8:14-18; 19:1-6; Rom. 1:11; 2 Tim. 1:6)

Seventh, they, along with the prophets, were used by God to write inspired scriptures. Although all of the apostles, and all of the prophets, did not write scriptures, they all taught by inspiration, and God used some of them to write inspired scriptures. If we have apostles and prophets today, at least some of them should write "more Bible."

The qualifications and the special work of the apostles were such as to make impossible a line of successors throughout the centuries. Who today was with Christ in His personal ministry? Who today can be guided into all the truth by direct inspiration? The apostles revealed all the truth in the first century. Jesus promised them that they would be guided into all the truth and, unless Jesus' promise failed (we know it did not), this had to be accomplished before the last of them died. Otherwise, they were not guided into all the truth. The apostles of Christ were a unique group, and as such are represented as having their names on the twelve foundations of the new Jerusalem in eternity. (Rev. 21:14)

MATTHIAS

Matthias became an apostle, for not only was he numbered with the apostles, but he was a part of the twelve apostles who are mentioned before the calling of Saul. (Acts 1:26; 6:2) What is unique about Matthias' case, which shows that no one would become his successor later? First, his selection was in fulfillment of prophecy. (Acts 1:20) Nowhere is it predicted that when the other apostles died others would take their places. Second, the office had been left vacant not by death but by the apostasy of Judas. (Acts 1:25) Third, the successor had to be one who had been with Christ in His personal ministry. (Acts 1:21-22) Fourth, this office was filled before the establishment of the church, and not afterwards. Fifth, this case also shows that it took more than being with Christ in His personal ministry to make one an apostle; for Barsabbas also had this qualification, but he was not elected to be an apostle. (Acts 1:23) The Lord had selected the apostles during His personal ministry, and He was asked, and He did, select the one whom He had chosen. (Acts 1:24-25)

PAUL

Saul's case was unusual, and he was especially the apostle of the Gentiles. (1 Cor. 15:8-9; Gal. 2:8-9) Christ selected him and he, therefore, was an apostle "not from men, neither through men, but through Jesus Christ. . . ." (Gal. 1:1) He saw the Lord. (Acts 22:14-15; 26:16-17; 1 Cor. 9:1) He was taught the gospel by revelation. (1 Cor. 15:1-3; Gal. 1:11-12) He confirmed it by a wide variety of miracles and thus manifested the signs of the apostle. (Rom. 15:19; 2 Cor. 12:12) He was not behind any of the apostles. (2 Cor. 11:5) He wrote inspired scripture. Furthermore, in listing the appearances of Christ after the resurrection, Paul said: "and last of all, as to the child untimely born, he appeared to me also." (1 Cor. 15:8)

OTHER INSPIRED MEN

In addition to the apostles, there were other inspired men, for Paul spoke of some who were prophets and teachers. (1 Cor. 12:28-29) These were not ordinary teachers, but were such by supernatural gifts of the Spirit. (1 Cor. 12:1, 11, 28-31) Ephesians also speaks of men who were apostles, prophets, evangelists, pastors, and teachers by gift; and these gifts were given after Christ's ascension. (Eph. 4:8, 11) Although we have those who teach, those who evangelize, those who are deacons, and those who are elders, we do not have any who are such by miraculous gifts. These gifts were given not in 1972 but after Christ ascended and during the time He was revealing and confirming the New Testament revelation. (Eph. 4:8; 1 Cor. 12:1, 4, 11, 31)

If we have the miraculous gifts today, we should have such individuals as the above; and men in whom are embodied, and through whom are manifested, the various gifts mentioned by the apostle Paul.

THEY DID THEIR WORK

The American Standard translation brings out, clearer than does the King James, the basic purpose of all these gifts and inspired individuals in whom the gifts were embodied; and through whom God worked in a supernatural way in the revelation and confirmation of the New Covenant. "And he gave some to be apostles; and some, prophets; and some, evangelists; and some, pastors and teachers; for the perfecting of the saints, unto the work of ministering, unto the building up of the body of Christ; till we all attain unto the unity of the faith, and of the knowledge of the Son of God, unto a fullgrown man, unto the measure of the stature of the fullness of Christ; that we may be no longer children, tossed to and fro and carried about with every wind of doctrine, by the sleight of men, in craftiness, after the wiles of error; but speaking truth in love, may grow up in all things into him, who is the head, even Christ; from whom all the body fitly framed and knit together, through that which every joint supplieth, according to the working in due measure of each several part, maketh the increase of the body unto the building up of itself in love." (Eph. 4:11-16)

Paul spoke of three things: (1) The perfecting of the saints. (2) The working of ministering. (3) The building up of the body of Christ so that Christians can mature. The inspired, and miraculously endowed, men revealed and confirmed the word of truth in order that these things might be accomplished. We have the word, which the miracles were designed to reveal and confirm, and with this same word of truth we carry on the work of ministry and build up the body of Christ.

Although the King James does not make a distinction, that word which it translates "for" three times is not the same word. The first "for" ("for the perfecting of the saints") is different from "unto the work of ministering, unto the building up of the body of Christ." Over one hundred and fifty years ago, James MacKnight translated this verse as follows: "And he appointed some, indeed apostles; and some prophets; and some evangelists; and some pastors and teachers; for the sake of fitting the saints for the work of the ministry, in order to the building of the body of Christ. . ." Paul's "meaning is, that the different orders of inspired teachers which he mentions, were appointed, and supernaturally endowed by God, for the purpose of giving the believing Jews and Gentiles such a complete knowledge of the gospel, as should qualify them for preaching it to unbelievers, and for building the body of Christ, by converting them. Accordingly, after the apostles and other inspired teachers were dead, their disciples spread the knowledge of the gospel everywhere. . . . All, in every age and country, who have devoted themselves to that work, have been fitted for it by them, in as much as from their writings alone they derive their knowledge of the gospel, by the preaching of which they build the body of Christ."

The inspired men perfected or equipped the saints, the church. This conveys the idea of "fitting," as MacKnight pointed out, and "properly signifies to place the parts of any machine or body in their proper order, and to unite them in such a manner as to render the machine or body complete. . . . In the metaphorical sense . . . signifies the fitting of a person, by proper instruction, for discharging any office or duty." Young's Analytical Concordance shows that the term "perfecting" is also translated "complete adjustment." G. R. Berry, in The Interlinear Literal Translation of the Greek New Testament, translates it "with a view to the perfecting of the saints; . . . ." James Moffatt translates it: "in order to fit his people for the work of service. . . ." The International Critical Commentary translates it: "with a view to the perfecting of the saints unto the work of ministering, unto the building up of the body of Christ."

In other words, these inspired gifts, and inspired men, were given in order to perfect or properly equip the church so that it could carry on the work of ministry and build up the body of Christ not only in numbers but also in maturity. The inspired men

BIBLICAL MIRACLES 17

accomplished their work through the truth which they revealed and confirmed. These gifts were exercised to convert unbelievers, and to edify the church. (1 Cor. 14:3, 19, 23, 24-25, 39)

By delivering, once for all, the faith unto the church (Jude 3), they equipped the church to carry on the work of ministry and the building up of the church. Their purpose having been accomplished, these gifts, and those in whom they were manifested, passed away. Through the complete truth which they delivered and confirmed (John 16:12-14; Jude 3), the church is equipped — although we may fail to use the equipment, just as did some in the first century — to carry on the work which God has ordained for it in evangelizing the world, doing good unto all men, and in edifying the saints.

Our apostles and prophets are in the foundation of the church and not in the walls or roof. We no more replace them each generation than we replace Christ. (Eph. 2:20) We have the apostles and prophets just like the rich man's brothers had Moses and the prophets — whom they were to hear — in that we have their writings. (Lk. 16:29-31, 24:27, 44)

ALL THE MIRACLES

Those who claim to repeat the miracles in the Bible need to prove that in their group they can work the entire range of the miracles. These include: (1) Miraculous creation of men and women. (2) Rod into serpent. (Ex. 3:20; 7:9) (3) Water into blood, and into wine. (Ex. 7:17; John 2:9) (4) Smiting a country with a plague of frogs. (Ex. 8:5) (5) Thick darkness such as in Egypt. (Ex. 10:21-23) (6) Death of the first born, but with the sparing of those who followed God's instructions. (Ex. 11:5) (7) Pillar of cloud by day and of fire by night. (Ex. 14:24) (8) Going through the sea on dry land. (Ex. 14:15; Joshua 3:13) (9) Clothes did not wax old. (Deut. 8:4; Neh. 9:21) (10) An unwilling prophet conveyed to his destiny via a great fish. (Jonah) (11) Leprosy cured after dipping seven times. (2 Kings 5:10) (12) Translation so one does not see death. (Gen. 5:24; Heb. 11:5; 2 Kings 2:1-11) (14) Miraculous transportation. (Acts 8:39-40) (15) Manna from heaven. (Ex. 16:4) (16) Meal and oil miraculously increased. (1 Kings 17:14) The same with reference to loaves and fishes. (John 6:5-14) (17) Someone turned into a pillar of salt. (Gen. 19:26) (18) Walking on the water. (Matt. 14:25, 29) (19) Unconsumed by the fire. (Dan. 3:20-26) (20) Sun and moon standing still. (Joshua 10:12) (21) Deliverance from prison. (Acts 5:19; 12:7; 16:26) (22) Missing members of body restored. (Matt. 15:30-

31; 18:8; Lk. 22:51) (23) The combination of the sound which all heard, of tongues which all understood, and cloven tongues which all saw. (Acts 2:1-4, 6, 8, 11, 33) (24) The resurrection of someone who has been dead for four days. (John 11:39-44)

ALL THE HEALING MIRACLES

Christ and the other miracle workers in the first century worked a wide variety of healing miracles. Christ wrought miracles on such as the following: (a) Blind. (Matt. 9:27-31; Mark 7:22-26) (b) Dumb. (Matt. 9:32-33; Mark 7:31-37) (c) Dropsy. (Luke 14:1-6) (d) Leper. (Luke 17:11-19) (e) Ear restored. (Luke 22:50-51) (f) Fever. (Matt. 8:14; John 4:46-54) (g) Palsied. (Matt. 8:5-7; 9:2) (h) Withered hand. (Matt. 12:10) (i) Bleeding. (Matt. 9:20) (j) Every sickness and disease. (Matt. 9:35) (k) Halt and maimed made whole. (Matt. 15:30; Luke 22:50-51) (l) Raised the dead. (John 11:39-44)

The apostles worked a wide variety of miracles of healing. (a) The man who was born lame walked immediately, having become perfectly sound, and it was known to multitudes in Jerusalem. (Acts 3:1-10; 4:13-16, 22) (b) All were healed who were brought to them. (Acts 5:12-16) (c) Palsied and lame. (Acts 8:6-7, 13) (d) Dead raised. (Acts 9:37, 40-42) (e) Not hurt by viper. (Acts 28:3-6) (f) Fever, dysentery, etc. (Acts 28:8-9)

If there are those with the gifts of healing today they should perform a wide variety of healing miracles.

ALL THE CHARACTERISTICS OF THE HEALING MIRACLES

They should also perform miracles which have the same characteristics as the miracles of Christ and the apostles. Are they matched by the modern "miracle" workers? (a) Instantaneous. (Matt. 8:3, 15; 9:27-30; 12:13, 22; Acts 3:7-8; 9:34; 13:11) Exceptions? No. Study closely. (Mark 8:23-25; Luke 17:12-14; John 4:50-52) (b) Faith not always required on part of one on whom the miracles were worked. (John 11:39; Acts 13:11-12; 16:18) (c) All, not just a few. (Matt. 4:24; 8:16; 9:35; 14:34-36; Luke 4:40; 9:11) (d) Organic disease, not merely functional disorders. (Matt. 15:30; Mark 14:47; Luke 17:11-19; Acts 3) (e) Public. (Matt. 12:9; 13-14; Acts 3:16; 4:21; 9:35) (f) Complete, whole, perfect. (Matt. 12:13; Acts 3:16, 4:9) (g) Acknowledged by enemies of Christ. (Matt. 12:13-14, 24; Acts 4:16; 16:18-19) (h) Not used to make money. (Matt. 10:8-10; Acts 3:6) (i) God-glorifying. (Acts 3:2-13) (j) Used

BIBLICAL MIRACLES

to support truth, not error. (Heb. 2:3-4) Not used to establish or perpetuate denominations. (k) Person healed did not have to be present. (Matt. 8:5-13) (l) Some miracles wrought over the protest of the individual. (Matt. 8:28; Mark 5:6-10; Luke 4:33) (m) Because of faith of others. (Matt. 8:8, 10, 13; John 4:50-53) (n) Jesus did not claim that it is God's will to heal all who believe, and then went about with a physical ailment Himself. (o) No preliminary investigations to weed out hard cases. (p) Jesus did not try and fail, and then insult them by saying that they did not have enough faith. The only case of failure, and this was before the baptism of the Spirit, was blamed on the ones who tried and failed. (Matt. 17:19-21) There was no such case after Pentecost. (Acts 1:8; 2:1-4) (q) Jesus did not say that he could not work miracles because unbelievers were present. (r) Jesus did not try and fail and then blame God by saying, I just pray, but cannot know whether God will work the miracle. (Compare Acts 1:8) Miracles proved the power of God. (Matt. 9:6; Mark 2:10; Luke 5:24) God did not refuse to work miracles through Christ and the apostles just because unbelievers were present! (s) Christ announced no special healing service. (t) His healings did not require a special "atmosphere." (u) God, when He saw fit, protected them miraculously. (Mark 16:17-18; Acts 12:7-11. Contrast Acts 12:2; Acts 28:3-6)

RAISING THE DEAD?

It is very rare that Pentecostals will even attempt to raise the dead. W. Ray Duncan wrote me on January 5, 1971 concerning a meeting in San Diego, California conducted by Ben Franklin at Christ's Center. Franklin is one of the preachers who has gone into Pentecostalism. One speaker told how some believers in Indonesia had raised 18 dead people. A close friend of brother Luker, who was with brother Duncan, had just died and Luker asked them to raise him from the dead. The leaders declined to go, but the next day three who were in the audience did go but they did not raise the dead. When someone took a picture, the Pentecostals manifested their tempers and wanted to know what they were going to do with the picture? "You are going to publish our FAILURE and wreck the faith of MILLIONS!" Luker said: "We offered to give them the picture if they would ASK for it! They hesitated! Cooled off! We have the pictures." (See these statements reproduced in Ira Y. Rice, Jr., *Contending for the Faith*, March 1971, pp. 2, 4-5)

TONGUES WERE LANGUAGES

The tongues in the New Testament were not ecstatic utterances, but human languages. *First,* the word for tongue was used not only to refer to the physical organ but to languages of men. (Acts 2:4, 11; Rev. 7:9; 5:9; 10:11; 11:9; 13:7; 14:6) *Second,* the tongues promised by Jesus were used to confirm the word. (Mk. 16:17, 20) How could ecstatic utterances, which anyone can utter, be a divine confirmation? *Third,* Mk. 16:20 briefly covers the signs done in Acts. Acts shows that the tongues were languages. (Acts 2:4, 6, 8, 11) The word was preached and confirmed in Corinth as well as in Jerusalem. (Acts 18:1-11; 1 Cor. 1:6-7; 2:4; 1 Cor. 14) There are no scriptural grounds for saying that the tongues were human languages in Acts 2, but ecstatic utterances in Corinth. Mark showed that the *same type of confirmation* was found wherever the word was preached. (Mk. 16:17-18, 20) *Fourth,* the word for interpret was used predominantly to refer to one language being translated into another language. *Fifth,* the reason that there was confusion in Corinth was that some were using the gift of tongues when no one who was there understood the language, and there was no interpreter present. (1 Cor. 14) *Sixth,* Paul in 1 Cor. 14:21 shows that reference is made to human languages. (Isa. 28:11) *Seventh,* the tongues were a sign to the unbeliever, but if he did not know the language which was used, and if there was no interpreter present, tongues could not be a sign to him. (1 Cor. 14:22-23) On Pentecost they were a sign because the people understood the languages. *Eighth,* Rom. 8:26-27 does not refer to our making unutterable groanings, but to what the Spirit Himself does. *Ninth,* no one in the New Testament was taught how to speak in tongues. However, many today tell the individual to utter sounds and then the Spirit will take over. Anyone can utter non-English sounds, and the more he does it the more fluent he becomes in it. This is the easiest thing in the world to deceive oneself into doing, for since it is not a language, and anyone can make sounds, the individual has no way to check on the tongue to show that it is inspired of God instead of being the result of man's own effort.

The fact that these people do not understand the nature of the tongues of Mk. 16:17-18 proves that they do not have this gift, nor do they have the gift of discernment or knowledge. They lack the other gifts also, for God would not give them gifts to confirm false teaching concerning tongues and other subjects. (Mk. 16:20)

In extremely rare cases, some have claimed to have heard a human language spoken. In the many millions of cases of people who have spoken in "tongues," it would be amazing if some sounds which they used did not sound like the words of some

BIBLICAL MIRACLES

human languages. In all the cases which linguists have recorded and investigated, none of them have been any known human language.

There have been cases where people have learned a language in childhood, have forgotten it, and then in an emotional situation or in a delirium have spoken the language. One girl, who had never learned Hebrew, heard the minister for whom she worked quote and read from the Old Testament in Hebrew. In a delirious condition she quoted some of these passages.

Could not unbelievers say that the apostles on Pentecost were unconsciously recalling the languages which they had heard in times past? *First,* it would have been a miracle, even if they had recalled these languages under emotional stimulation, to have recalled just those languages which were the native tongues of the different people who assembled. (Acts 2:4, 6, 8, 11) *Second,* on Pentecost tongues were not the only evidence of supernatural power. The sound and the tongues, parting asunder like as of fire, were also present. (Acts 2:1-4, 33) Furthermore, the apostles reasoned with them from Scriptures, appealed to their own knowledge that Jesus had wrought miracles (Acts 2:22), and set forth their own personal witness to the resurrected Christ. (Acts 2:32) *Third,* there is no proof that the apostles had ever learned these languages.

One person, before he changed after being in the tongues movement for years, asked me: Do you think Jesus would have let the people analyze what He said like some of us want to analyze the modern tongues speakers and miracle workers? *First,* in the very nature of the case, when one claims to work miracles he is inviting people to scrutinize closely what he does. Jesus never expected anyone to accept something without weighing it. Therefore, through Paul, Jesus said to prove all things and hold fast that which is good. (1 Thess. 5:21) *Second,* Jesus invited doubting Thomas to make a close investigation which involved touch. (John 20:24-29) *Third,* Luke traced things accurately. (Lk. 1:3) *Fourth,* since there are, even according to Pentecostals, those who falsely claim to work miracles, how is one to decide whether a miracle is wrought without closely examining the evidence? *Fifth,* how are we to obey 1 John 4:1 unless we test or prove claims? Christians were commended for examining, or trying, those who claim to be apostles. (Rev. 2:2) Men were commended for examining the scriptures to see whether what Paul preached was so. (Acts 17:11) How much more should we examine those who claim to be sent of God with miraculous gifts today?

FINANCIAL MIRACLE?

One of the "miracles" Pat Boone stresses in *A New Song* was being rescued financially from a disastrous situation which involved around two million dollars. (*A New Song*, pp. 159-162) However, I did not think it was a miracle. Some of his financial advisors had been working hard on the problem, and had contacted the man who finally bought the ball club. In April 1971 the author was in Ontario, and heard a tape recording of an interview which Pat had a day or so before on a radio or TV program in Hamilton, Ontario. Pat mentioned the financial miracle. We wondered why he forgot to mention that earlier in 1971 he had filed under the Federal bankruptcy act, with reference to the Wendell West Company in which he was a partner. Many millions were lost in that venture, but Pat failed to mention this lack of a miracle which was far greater than the financial "miracle". (See newspaper clippings reproduced in Ira Y. Rice, Jr., *Contending for the Faith*, March 1971, pp. 3-4. I also have clippings)

I am confident that Pat has explained this huge failure to himself in such a way that it does not undermine his faith in the "miraculous" in a much smaller financial matter. The author wants to mention here that he and Pat are on the best of terms personally. Each has a warm spot in his heart for the other. He has gone beyond my fellowship but not beyond my love. When the author was in the hospital in October-November 1971 Pat had special prayer for him at a service he was attending in Nashville, sent the author flowers, and phoned him. Although I cannot agree with the doctrines which he has taken up, Pat is a warm-hearted and loveable person.

MIRACLES?

Obviously, the author has not seen everything but the so-called miracles which he has seen, and on which he has been able to check, have not matched the miracles of the Bible. Furthermore, a "miracle" which he witnessed in Oakland, California — at a meeting of Mrs. Bebe H. Patton — was quite different in the write-up from what he saw happen, and on which he checked two weeks later by visiting the person who was supposedly healed but still was unhealed.

In the spring of 1972 one of the author's students who had been associated with Pentecostalism for years as a believer in it, said that he had heard of the healing of incurable diseases, but he had never seen any of them. All was "hearsay." He had seen many attempts but no successes. His cousin is paralyzed from the waist down as a result of polio. He said she had asked more than once to see Oral Roberts, but when the nature of her case was known, she was not allowed to appear.

WHY SOME CLAIM MIRACLES?

The modern "miracles" which I have witnessed have not been miracles. A man came to see me in Searcy. He told me of many amazing things which he had seen and done, and that the Lord had directed him to me. He prayed for the healing of my broken wrist. There was no change. A week later he saw me, and the cast was off my arm. He thought a miracle had taken place. I told him my wrist and fingers were still stiff, and that before he came to see me the doctor had already said he planned to take the cast off in a couple of weeks or so.

Some of the reports of miracles are based on the following: *First,* many people have functional, not organic, disorders. When they think they are better they are better. The healer convinces them that they are better and they believe it and feel better. Many cases of healings of this type are found in Dr. F. Dunbar's *Emotions and Bodily Changes.* The power of the mind is great. *Second,* in some cases improvement is only temporary but they viewed it as a miracle. *Third,* in some cases, where "healers" were not involved, cases of cancer have been cured. For some reason, unknown to science, certain bodily processes reversed or stopped the development of the cancer. *Fourth,* some of them view a gradual recovery as a miracle. While we should be grateful for recovery, let us not confuse something which is gradual, and an affirmative answer to prayer, with the position that we have the power to say: In the name of Jesus of Nazareth, walk. (Acts 1:8; 3:6) *Fifth,* sometimes something may coincide in point of time and be viewed as a miracle. In October 1971 my heart had been beating for several hours at 160 beats per minute. A mechanism which someone in Memphis had invented was being used to detect certain heart sounds which would otherwise be overshadowed by other sounds. A doctor touched the machine, and while he was doing something with reference to it, reached over and touched me. My pulse immediately became normal. He had not laid hands on me to heal me, and when I had fast beats later they did not stop under such circumstances. Of course, I was extremely grateful that the beat slowed, and thanked God it did, but it was not a miracle. In fact, he was surprised, and I understand that some doctors asked him what words did he say when he touched me! *Sixth,* some people testify they have been healed because they have been convinced that if they claim the healing in faith they will receive it. They claim it, so they have received it. Therefore, they glorify God for the healing. But they still have the symptoms. The symptoms have been put there by the devil to shake their faith in the healing!! If they believe the devil rather than God they will lose their healing!! So they praise God for the healing although every symptom indicates they have not been healed.

SHIFTING THE APPROACH

If one has the power, let him demonstrate it. Christ did not argue that He could raise the dead, and then fail to do it. *Miracles are the subject for demonstration, not just argumentation.* If you can do it, why argue about it, and if you cannot do it, arguments will not prove that you can do it. For centuries it has been considered that the miracles, and the revelation of additional truths, ceased in the apostolic age. Those who affirm that they have the power today must prove it. *The laboring oar is in their hands.* It is not so much that we must prove they cannot, as that they must prove they can; although we are willing to show they do not do what Christ and the apostles did. So let us ask them to prove they are working miracles. Let them demonstrate or desist from their claims.

A. W. L. Jenkins in Mississippi claimed that God had spoken to him, and he said he was going to walk on the water of the Ross Barnett Reservoir in May 1972. He cancelled the walk after he said someone shot him in the leg. As the title of an article by Robert R. Taylor, Jr. put it: "Water Proof But Not Bullet Proof." (*Words of Truth,* Jasper, Alabama, June 30, 1972) Of course, as Taylor brought out, he was neither.

Chapter II

Some Characteristics of the Movement

What are some of the characteristics of the Pentecostal movement in the church? It is not being suggested that every one in the movement has all these characteristics, but they are found in the movement. Those who have these characteristics have the same type of signs that those have who do not share some of the *same characteristics.*

THE THEATRICAL AND DRAMATIC

Pentecostalism is a movement which often involves the theatrical and the dramatic. Some of the denominational leaders in Pentecostalism are very flamboyant and melodramatic. One such person had a lot of influence on the brother to whom Olan Hicks wrote as follows: "You are a student of drama, with a highly developed capacity to feel a scene, even though it is entirely fictional. You have a keenly developed capacity to appreciate the dramatic and to reflect a living response to the directives of a good author." He urged this brother to pick out the facts and separate them from the melodrama. "You don't have to consult the Bible about whether you can raise the dead or speak in a language you haven't learned. You just try it and see. Elaborate adjectives and melodramatic descriptions do not change facts, they just change minds."

They will take some coincidence, such as happens many times in the lives of all of us, and view it as a supernatural manifestation. They make something natural sound as if it were supernatural. They often explain supernaturally something which can be explained psychologically, and which takes place in various religions and even in the lives of some non-religious people.

MINIMIZING THE MIND

Pentecostalism as a movement tends to minimize the mind. One student wrote my wife that while he was at a certain college he was deeply involved in the tongues movement. When he saw my book on the shelf by Pat's, he called mine "sheer intellectualism." Pat minimized the mind. (*Pat Boone and the Gift of Tongues,* pp. 23-41)

We have dealt with this in the second section of this book which reviews Sherrill's *They Speak With Other Tongues.* Only brief comments will be made here. *First,* the Pentecostals must use their mind to decide that the gifts are for us, to learn how to seek them, to conclude that they have sought and received them, and to evaluate the evidence which they think proves that they now have one or more gifts. *Second,* although the gospel is not the product of the mind (1 Cor. 2:10-13), it is addressed to the mind. (1) Love for God includes loving Him with the mind. (Matt. 22:37-38) (2) Through the use of the mind, man can learn of God's existence. (Rom. 1:20-25; Psa. 14:1) (3) Faith comes by hearing God's word, which includes the presentation of evidence. (John 5:32-47; 20:30-31; Rom. 10:17) (4) The apostles reasoned with the people. (Acts 9:29; 17:2-4; 18:4; 19:9; 18:28) Peter presented the evidence from prophecy (Acts 2:17-21, 25-28, 30, 34, 35), from Christ's miracles (2:22), from the resurrection (2:32) and from the miracles on Pentecost wherein something was heard, seen and done, i.e., they spoke with other *tongues* after the sound as of a rushing mighty *wind* and the tongues like as of *fire.* (Acts 2:1-4, 6, 8, 11, 33) He drew the conclusion that: "Let all the house of Israel *therefore know assuredly,* that God hath made him both Lord and Christ, this Jesus whom ye crucified." (Acts 2:36) (5) The Bereans were commended for listening and studying, and this led to faith. (Acts 17:11-12) (6) We must use our mind to learn Christ's word in the Bible, to prove all things and hold fast the good, to be able to give answer, and to contend for the faith. (1 Thess. 5:21; 1 Pet. 3:15; Jude 3; Eph. 3:4; 5:17) 1 Cor. 14 emphasizes that the assembly was an exercise in futility unless the mind was instructed. We also must use the mind to apply Christ's principles to concrete situations.

Zeal and emotions do not substitute for knowledge. (Rom. 10; 1-4; Eph. 3:4) We must use our minds in order to listen to and understand the Bible which is God's voice, the prophet's voice, the Spirit's voice, and the authoritative word. (Matt. 22:31; Lk. 16:29-31; Acts 13:27; Heb. 10:15; Rev. 2:1, 7; 1 Cor. 14:37. See the additional discussions in *Pat Boone and the Gift of Tongues,* pp. 23-41. Dub McClish, "A New Attack on 'Human Reason' " *Firm Foundation,* June 13, 1972, pp. 371, 380)

LONG ON ARGUMENT BUT SHORT ON DEMONSTRATION

The Pentecostal movement is long on argument but short on

SOME CHARACTERISTICS OF THE MOVEMENT 27

demonstration. *First,* they argue that if one asks in faith he can receive the gifts, and yet they fail to demonstrate all of the gifts. In fact, with reference to some of them they do not even try.

Second, they claim the gift of tongues, and utter sounds not spoken by men instead of speaking in foreign languages which they have not learned. (Acts 2:4, 6, 8, 11)

Third, after applying John 14:12 to miraculous works, they refuse to do greater miracles than did Jesus. They do not even try to walk on the water or miraculously multiply the loaves and fishes.

Fourth, they apply to themselves the promise of Acts 1:8, and excuse their failures by saying that the power is not with them but with God. They say that they do not have power, therefore they are not to be blamed when they try and fail. Although the power was from God, the apostles and certain others on whom they laid hands had power. (1) Christ promised that the apostles would receive power when the Spirit came on them. (Acts 1:2-3, 5, 8) (2) They did receive power when this happened. They spoke in other languages (Acts 2:1-4, 6, 8, 11), God wrought miracles "by their hands" (14:3), "through" them (2:43; 15:12), "God wrought special miracles by the hands of Paul" (19:11), Paul spoke of the miracles "Christ wrought through me" (Rom. 15:18-19), and the Spirit was imparted in a miraculous way through the laying on of the apostles' hands. (Acts 8:17-19; 19:1-6; Rom. 1:11; 2 Tim. 1:6) (3) God gave the gifts, but He gave them to men. (1 Cor. 12:8-11, 29-30) (4) If God inspires men today, and gives them power, He would let them know when they were to work a miracle so that they could not try and fail and then blame, as it were, the failure on God! (5) Oral Roberts used Lk. 24:49, Acts 1:8; 2:4 to prove that when you are baptized with the Spirit, "you are supernaturally endued with power from on high." ". . . power that dwells inside you and which you can feel inside." (*The Baptism With the Holy Spirit,* pp. 2-3) Roberts views his hands as an extension of the hands of Christ. (*Commentary,* p. 648) He also claims to tell people "exactly how you may receive your healing." (*Abundant Life,* August, 1970, pp. 6-9)

Fifth, they apply to themselves all the promises of Mark 16:17-18 and then fail to demonstrate them all. (1) There is an extended discussion of this passage in James D. Bales, *Miracles or Mirages?* pp. 233-257. (2) The so-called modern miracle workers do not do all the things mentioned in Matt. 16:17-18 and embraced in Mk. 16:20; which covers all the miracles done by the miracle workers in the first century. (3) The promise of Mk. 16:17-20 is limited by the purpose and duration of miracles as revealed in this and other passages.

Oral Roberts teaches that the serpents in Mk. 16:18 are enemies such as in Lk. 10:19. (*Commentary,* pp. 646-647) There is no more evidence that this meant figurative serpents than there is that drinking any deadly thing meant drinking in false doctrine. Paul was not hurt by an actual viper. (Acts 28:3-6)

Anthony A. Hoekema wrote: "As we examine the Greek text of Mark 16:18, however, we find that, though the statement about drinking poison is put in a conditional form ('If they drink any deadly thing it shall not hurt them'), the statement about taking up serpents is not put in a conditional form, but is in the future indicative: 'They shall take up serpents,' as is the statement about tongues: 'they shall speak with new tongues', . . . If the speaking with new tongues is to be taken as a sign which confirms believers in their faith, why must we not further conclude that taking up serpents is also to function as such a sign? There is as much reason for accepting the one sign as the other, since in both cases the Greek verb is in the future indicative . . ." (*What About Tongues Speaking?,* pp. 55-56) If we should have the sign of tongues, why not the sign of taking up serpents?

Roberts believes he can lay hands on the sick and they will recover. (Mk. 16:18) "I know that I have a command of God to lay my hands upon the people, and God uses my hands. I look on them, not as endowed with any special virtue or power, but as an extension of the hands of Christ. When I touch someone I try to envision my hands as an extension of the hands of Christ. I see Him touching you. And when He touches you, you are made whole — in soul, mind and body!" (*Commentary,* p. 648) If Mk. 16:18 applies to him, and if his hands are extensions of the hands of Christ, and if you are healed when Christ touches you, why does Roberts have so many failures? Jesus said: "They shall recover." (Mk. 16:18) The author received a letter in July 1970 from a cripple who told him of a spastic who went through Roberts' healing line and is still a spastic. If, in effect, Roberts' hands are an extension of the hands of Christ, there is special virtue or power in them. He should know this, if he knows that God gave him a command to lay on hands and if God uses his hands.

STRONG LANGUAGE

There are some who view a person as unspiritual if he uses strong language concerning error and especially concerning those

SOME CHARACTERISTICS OF THE MOVEMENT

who have embraced and propagated error. I believe one can use strong language concerning error, when the error is serious, and that there are even times when one can use strong language — though we should try to be very sure when it is time for such — concerning those who teach the error. Paul used strong language in Galatians 2.

One Pentecostal among us, whom I have been assured is a very gentle person by one who knows him, has said that those who reject the gifts for today do not trust the Lord; that they put evil for good and good for evil; that they have waxed gross; that they have a strong delusion; that they do not believe in the truth and choose wickedness instead; that they pass scriptures on the subject of gifts through a filter of unbelief; that they are an evil and adulterous generation who seek signs — even though they accept and are satisfied with the signs given in the Bible, *although he is not satisfied with them but seeks more signs today;* that they have not been born of water and the Spirit; that they have not received the Spirit; that they have placed themselves outside the convicting power of the Spirit; that they "have believed a lie that continually casts a shadow of death across" their path to God; and that they are scribes and Pharisees who will not enter the kingdom and will not allow those who would enter in to enter.

We ought to be willing to study to see whether these passages apply to us, but we are in no wise upset because this person thinks they apply to us! However, we would ask any readers who view us as being harsh legalists, and view those like him as being gentle and spiritual men who do not say harsh things about brethren, to remember what he has said of those who differ with him on this subject.

At least three persons who advocate the gifts wrote me harsh letters concerning my book on *Pat Boone and the Gift of Tongues.* They had not read the book, but they made some harsh judgments concerning me and the book. When I wrote and asked them if the Spirit guided them in these things, they apologized. To me, the explanation is simple. These people are often guided by their impulses. Since they do not accept the Bible as the absolute standard, but accept their personal experience and gifts as also authoritative, they have a difficult time distinguishing between their own impulses and what the Spirit would have them do. This is the reason that some of these people can be very quick to judge one's motives. However, when their attention is called to these matters, in some cases their impulses change, they have taken some time now to deliberate, and they may change their tune.

DECEPTION

In some cases, Pentecostalism in our midst has been characterized by deception. This is all the more serious since they usually think that the Spirit has guided them into such a course. Therefore, they do not view it as deception. There are those who will not make known their convictions publicly, but will build cells in a congregation or college. They are careful as to whom they invite into their meetings. Some of them rationalize and blame their deception on us. They say that if they make known their position they will be crucified by brethren. It is not crucifixion when brethren refuse to support or endorse those who undermine them! In one case a missionary continued to receive support, after being converted to Pentecostalism, and finally he tried with some others to take over the church building.

John L. Sherrill became a tongues speaker, and he raised the question as to how to share it with others. (1) Should he remain in the Episcopal church in suburban New York and preach the baptism in the Spirit and the gift of tongues? (2) Should he leave "his church and join a Pentecostal group"? (3) Should he stay, and say nothing except when it comes up naturally, and "keep company with Pentecostals on the side"? He said that a tongues speaker forgot how long it took to convert him, and "far too often in his enthusiasm he forgot basic strategy, and instead of being able to communicate, his very boldness blocked his ability to reach others."

Sherrill decided on the third course, but wrote: "Yet, this is not a good solution either. If I believe in the importance of the Baptism in the Holy Spirit, as I do, do I not have an obligation to talk about it wherever and whenever I can?" (*They Speak With Other Tongues,* Old Tappan, N.J.: Fleming H. Revell Co., 1968, pp. 134-135)

A few years ago a friend of the author visited a meeting of the Full Gospel Business Men's Fellowship. He reported that the audience was told that when they received the baptism of the Spirit, and spiritual gifts, they should not leave their denominations but should remain in them and influence them from within. A Roman Catholic priest, Joseph Orsini wrote an article entitled: "Stay Where You Are." (*Logos Journal,* Jan.-Feb. 1972, p. 18) If these individuals make known their change, they are not being dishonest, but if they work behind the scenes — while leaving the impression that they do not adhere to these doctrines — they are being dishonest. The Holy Spirit would not be a party to such deception. Although the individual could be so confused that he

SOME CHARACTERISTICS OF THE MOVEMENT

was not making a conscious effort to deceive, the Holy Spirit would not be confused and He would know what was taking place. Neither miraculously, nor through the Bible, would He lead an individual to do such a thing.

Of course, we are not talking about individuals who are struggling with a problem concerning miraculous gifts, but of individuals who think they have them but fail to make known to their brethren their present position.

Some time ago the author talked with a friend who has become involved in the tongues movement, and who thinks that the other gifts also are for us today. The author told this friend that if this was a conviction, and not just a problem concerning which he was confused, he was obligated to let brethren know where he stands. If he did not, the author indicated that after he had studied with him, and if neither one of us changed, the author would make it known. This friend was told that we were not charging him with having bad motives but that what he had done so far indicated that he did not have the miraculous guidance of the Spirit. The author pointed out that: *First,* a prominent brother, who had defended him but would not have defended him in the way that he did if he had known the full truth about his views, in effect was being left out on a limb. It was not fair to such brethren to leave them in the dark. He said he had not thought of this before. *Second,* we mentioned that brethren who invited him to speak did so, in my judgment, because they thought that he had been misrepresented. Although he has been misrepresented on some matters, on certain matters he has not been misrepresented. If brethren knew his position, and still wanted to invite him, they at least would know what they were doing.

The brother said that he had viewed the gift of tongues, and some of these other things, as means of private devotion and edification and not as something on which one was obligated to take a public stand. He said that he did tell people when they asked him about it, and that in it all he was depending on the leading of the Holy Spirit. With this confusion in his thinking, the author could see how he could do this in all good conscience, while one who was not so confused would be guilty of the conscious deception of brethren.

Of course, I realize that one does not go around broadcasting continuously his position on all possible subjects, but when one's position is a matter of public concern, and brethren are both attacking and defending, one is obligated to take a stand if he has a stand; or to tell why he has no stand.

This brother was confused when he said that tongues were primarily for private devotion. Primarily they were to be used in the proclamation and confirmation of the gospel. They were to help convert unbelievers, and when used in the assembly they should edify the brethren. (Mk. 16:17, 20; Acts 2:6, 8, 11; 1 Cor. 14:22, 15-19, 27, 28) If he had what he thought he had, the Spirit in him would know the purpose of these gifts. The Spirit would not leave him with the impression that they were primarily for private devotion. If the Spirit did not tell him this in a direct revelation, He would tell him this through some other inspired man. As a matter of fact, the Spirit has already told us this in the Bible.

In not taking a public stand the brother was not following the guidance of the Holy Spirit. Regardless of how good his motives, the Spirit would not lead him into a position which, in effect even if not by design, deceived brethren. The Spirit speaks to us through His word. The only word of the Spirit which we have is the Bible.

One Baptist minister said nothing for two months about his conversion to the tongues movement. He said he, his wife, and the one who had laid hands on them (a lady who was an Episcopalian), prayed "that God would give us wisdom to share our experience with the church in the most constructive way." They first shared it with small groups. (*Logos,* May-June, 1972, p. 47)

What a striking contrast between being quiet about having the gift of tongues, and organizing cells, and what happened when the apostles got the real gift of tongues!! *First,* since it was to be one of the signs to convince the unbelieving world, it could not be done in secret. (Mk. 16:17-18, 20; 1 Cor. 14:22) *Second,* what happened the first time the apostles spoke in tongues? Did they do it secretly because they were in a city which was actually hostile to Jesus and not just opposed to tongues? Did they refuse to make it public because they were going to teach people who had crucified the Son of God? (Acts 2:36) No. They did it publicly. The Holy Spirit and God clearly identified who they were. (a) There was a sound as of a rushing mighty wind which brought the audience to the place where they could hear and see the tongues speakers. (Acts 2:2, 6) (b) There were tongues, parting asunder like as of fire, which sat upon each of the speakers and clearly identified them. (2:3) (c) They spoke in tongues in the presence of an audience of unbelievers, and the audience heard — every man in the language wherein he was born. (2:4, 6, 8, 11) The apostles did not secretly speak in tongues over a period of

SOME CHARACTERISTICS OF THE MOVEMENT 33

time, and then surface publicly after they had secretly influenced some people. The very first time they spoke in tongues they spoke publicly.

We are not suggesting that a person who is struggling with the problem of tongues, but is not convinced that he has it and is not advocating it, should publicly parade his problems before everyone. He should seek help and try to settle the matter scripturally. However, he who believes in and advocates tongues and does it secretly shows that he is not guided by the same Spirit who guided the apostles, nor does he have the same gift, nor have it for the same purpose.

TURNING LIMITED PROMISES INTO UNLIMITED

Pentecostalism often turns limited, or qualified, promises into unlimited promises. It is a well known principle of Bible study that the whole of the revealed truth about a subject is not contained in one passage unless there is only one passage on that particular subject. One passage may show that another passage is limited or qualified. For example, we are saved by grace, but this is not the total truth about salvation. If it were, man would not need to believe. On the other hand, although we are saved by faith, of what value would faith be if it were not for the Lamb of God who died for our sins? We are told to teach others (Matt. 28:19), but there are exceptions for we are told not to cast our pearls before swine. (Matt. 7:6) Some other illustrations are: (a) Are we to give to everyone who asks? (Matt. 5:42) No. (2 Thess. 3:10, 15) (b) Are we forbidden to work for our food? (John 6:27) No. One is to work and eat his own bread (2 Thess. 3:12), provide for one's self and help others. (Eph. 4:28) These people in John 6:26-29 were seeking Christ for the wrong purpose. The sign of the multiplication of the food should have led them to recognize that Christ had a message from God to which they should hearken. "Instead of seeing," Lange wrote, "in the bread the sign, they had seen in the sign only the bread." The work of God which they wanted was physical in nature, and the work which God wanted to do for them had to do with faith in God and Christ. Jesus was not discussing whether one should work for a living. (c) One may pray, and not receive, because he has wrong purposes in mind. (Jas. 4:3) (d) How one treats one's wife can hinder his prayers. (1 Pet. 3:7) (e) There is mercy with the Lord, but no amount of faith can enable us to pray away the law of sowing and reaping. (Gal. 6:7-9) We must change the sowing in order to change the reaping. (f) Wives are to submit to their husbands in all things (Eph. 5:24), but not if it leads them to disobey God. (Acts 5:29) (g) In the very context of the promise that they would receive what they asked in faith, Jesus showed that it took more than one's personal conviction. One would not be forgiven when he prayed for forgiveness, if he did not forgive. (Mk. 11:25) (h) Matt. 7:1 is not unlimited for if it were we could not distinguish between a beam and a mote, the broad and the narrow, the true and false prophets, or the good and evil tree. How could we be fruit inspectors if we could not make any judgments? (Matt. 7:15-20)

What are some of the passages which the Pentecostals treat as if they were unlimited when in reality they are limited? One wrote that: "According to John, Jesus made some specific statements about what *a person who believed* in him could expect." *First,* "He said that *the one who believed* in him would do the works that he did." (Italics by J.D.B.) Does he raise the dead, walk on the water, multiply the loaves and the fishes? He does not live far from the Atlantic Ocean. Let him demonstrate his faith, or show his unbelief if he fails, by walking on the ocean. Jesus also said that they would do *greater works.* What greater miracles, than Christ did, does he do? If he does not, how can he be consistent with his own position and claim that he is a believer? Christ is here talking with the apostles. (John 13; Matt. 26:20-26) He calls on them to believe (John 14:9-22), and promises them that they shall do the works which He has done and even greater works. Since the apostles did not do greater miracles than Jesus, unless speaking in tongues is a greater miracle than walking on the water, the greater works must refer to other types of works. What greater works did they do *because Jesus went unto the Father?* (John 14:12) Although their miracles were not superior in nature to those of Christ, their spiritual work was greater in that it was based on Christ's work as the Lamb who had already died for our sins, and His reign as king and high priest. (Acts 2:34-36; Heb. 1:3, 13)

What were some of the ways in which their works were greater? (a) Geographically. (b) Nationally and racially. (Eph. 2:13-19) (c) Christ taught the gospel in promise, and they in fulfillment. (d) Numerically. (e) Longer duration in time. (f) Christ taught that His reign was at hand (Matt. 4:17, 23), while they proclaimed that He now reigns. (Acts 2:34-36; Col. 1:13) Of course, their work was really His work through them.

Second, some believe that Jesus promised each believer the Spirit as the Counselor to be with him forever and "that this

Counselor would teach the believer all things." If this applies to people today as believers, each has an inspired remembrance of what Jesus taught in His personal ministry, and the Spirit guides them by inspiration into all the truth. (John 14:26; 16:12-14) They learn God's will not through perspiration (study) but through direct inspiration. John 14:26 does not teach that they would be taught all things by the Spirit through the written word. The believers in whom his promise was fulfilled were inspired and gave us the written word. What do people today know about the teaching of Christ, the apostles, and prophets which they did not learn from the written word or from someone who learned it from the written word? On their own logic, they are unbelievers unless they learn all things by direct inspiration, for John 14:26 refers to direct inspiration.

Third, some apply to all believers today the promises of Mk. 16:17-18. (a) Do they cast out demons? (b) Do they speak with new tongues? These were languages. (Mk. 16:20; Acts 2:4, 6, 8, 11) Are they unbelievers because they make sounds which are not the languages of the people who hear them? (c) Do they take up serpents? (d) Will any deadly thing they drink in no wise hurt them? (e) Do they lay hands on the sick, and they recover? It did not say that the sick on whom they laid hands had to believe. It did not say that some would recover and that some would not recover.

Fourth, some apply the promise of power in Acts 1:8 to themselves in that they apply it to all believers. Jesus was speaking to the apostles. (Acts 1:2, 6, 13) Jesus said: "But *ye shall receive power, when the Holy Spirit is come upon you:* and ye shall be my witnesses both in Jerusalem, and in all Judea and Samaria, and unto the uttermost part of the earth." (Acts 1:8) The apostles were the select group of witnesses. Although two disciples had been with them from the baptism of John unto the day of the ascension, only one was chosen to become a witness with the other apostles of the resurrected Christ. (Acts 1:21-22) On Pentecost Peter, standing up with the eleven, said that they were witnesses of the resurrection. (Acts 2:14, 32) These were the ones, and not disciples today, who were told to wait in Jerusalem until they receive power. (Acts 1:2, 4, 8) They received power on Pentecost. Through their word they continue to bear witness to Jesus. (Compare Lk. 16:29-31; Acts 13:26-27; 1 John 1:1-4) If this promise applies to us today, it should be fulfilled as it was then. Where is the sound as of a rushing mighty wind? the tongues like as of fire which sit upon each of us when the promise is fulfilled?

where are the foreign languages spoken by inspiration? where is the preaching by direct inspiration of the Spirit? and where is the necessity of our continuing steadfastly in the doctrine of the people today in whom these things are supposedly fulfilled? (Acts 2:1-4, 6, 8, 11, 42) It is a striking thing that, after applying this promise to themselves, some of these individuals maintain that they do not have power. However, the passage promises that they would receive power, and if the promise applies to them they must have the power.

Fifth, some use the following statement of Jesus as proof that if we ask in faith we shall receive tongues and/or other gifts. "And all things, whatsoever ye shall ask in prayer, believing, ye shall receive." (Matt. 21:18-22) Does this mean that if we ask in faith we shall receive the miraculous gifts? (1) Jesus was speaking to the disciples. (Mk. 11:1, 12, 15, 19, 20, 22-24) (2) He did deal with the miraculous for at His word the disciples had seen the fig tree wither immediately. (Matt. 21:19-20) (3) The apostles and some others had a gift of faith which involved the miraculous; but not everyone had this faith. (1 Cor. 12:9) However, without love the faith that moved mountains was profitless. (1 Cor. 13:2) (4) As far as we know the apostles never miraculously cast a mountain into the sea (Matt. 21:21), so evidently it was not God's will that this be done miraculously. (5) If this passage is unlimited, why do modern "miracle" workers fail so often to work miracles? (6) Why have they *never* cast a mountain into the sea? Surely they have faith as "a grain of mustard seed;" which was a proverb for something very small. If they have a very small faith, they must be able to miraculously move mountains; if they have rightly interpreted Jesus' statement. (Matt. 21:18-21) Instead of arguing about this passage, they should demonstrate; but they move no more mountains than does the author. If they move the first mountain, and if their teaching harmonizes with the New Testament, the author will be encouraged to try to move the next mountain. (7) "A grain of mustard seed" was a proverbial expression for something very small (Matt. 17:20) and moving a mountain could indicate something tremendous. The apostles did great miracles, but they never literally moved a mountain. John did no miracles, but spiritually speaking he moved mountains. (Isa. 40:4-5; Lk. 3:5; John 10:41) (8) Matt. 17:20-21 is limited even by those who argue as if it is unlimited. They do not move mountains. *The unmoved mountain stands between them and their arguments.* Even when miraculous power was granted, it was limited by God's will. We do not have miraculous power today, so the passage was limited by the purposes and

SOME CHARACTERISTICS OF THE MOVEMENT

duration of the miracles. The faith has been revealed and confirmed. No matter how strong our personal conviction about our receiving the very thing we ask for, we must remember that the decisive factor is God's will and what God has promised — not what we or others have promised ourselves. (Rom. 4:20-21; 1 John 5:14) (9) Some come to doubt whether they have the Spirit, and they may feel they generated the tongues themselves. Some of them are told that, after His baptism, Jesus was tempted. (Sherrill, *They Speak With Other Tongues,* 127-128) Jesus was not tempted to doubt that He had the Spirit or that He was the Messiah. (Matt. 4) Instead of re-examining their position in the light of the Bible, these individuals believe this doubt is of the devil and must be put away through faith in God. Of course, it is difficult to reason with people who view your arguments from the Bible as temptation from the devil! (10) If one can receive one gift simply by asking in faith, why cannot he receive all of the gifts? To argue otherwise is to maintain that the passage is limited. Therefore, the only reason each of them does not have all of the gifts, including that of the apostleship with its authority (1 Cor. 14:37; Acts 2:42), is because they do not have enough faith. (11) If the passage is unlimited why not ask for the gift of inspiration to enable them to write an inspired commentary on the entire Bible; especially on the difficult scriptures? (12) This attitude, that one shall receive the gifts if he asks in faith, makes it very easy for one to be deceived. He thinks he receives the gifts when he seeks them in faith, and having sought in faith he has received them. Those who have the gifts ought to use them, so they use them. With reference to some of the gifts, they cannot keep from deceiving themselves with this approach. If they can make sounds at all, they can make sounds in other than English. They think this is speaking in tongues. If they can talk about religion, they can call this the gift of prophecy. Irenaeus (A.D. 120-202) tells of a heretic named Marcus who taught women to prophesy. "Open thy mouth, speak whatsoever occurs to thee, and thou shalt prophesy." And they did! (*Ante-Nicene Fathers,* Vol. I, pp. 334-335)

These passages illustrate how the Pentecostals turn limited promises into unlimited ones.

IF BELIEVE STRONGLY ENOUGH?

Although there is room for growth in faith on the part of all of us, this does not mean that we can accomplish literally everything if we believe strongly enough. In 1958 Will Nicholson in

Alcoa, Tennessee was interviewed. He built a house to last 1,000 years because he thought he would live that long. At the time he was 81 but his faith was so strong he believed that he would live until the second coming and then live with Christ for 1,000 years on earth. His wife died, and he said: "Her faith just wasn't strong enough." (*The Commercial Appeal,* Memphis, Nov. 2, 1958) Some tongues speakers told Herman Otten that if a person's faith was really strong he would neither get sick nor die. (*The Christian News,* May 31, 1971, p. 2) A man in Tennessee had faith that a copperhead bite would not hurt him, but when he was bitten his arm swelled. He was all right in a few days. A rattlesnake bit him and four days later the swelling had gone down. Regardless of his faith he was hurt. (*The Commercial Appeal,* July 1, 1971) A woman handled a snake at a religious meeting. It bit her and she was told that if she called a doctor she would lose faith; so she rejected help and died as the congregation prayed. (*Gospel Advocate,* Oct. 18, 1951, p. 658) In what has been called the Jesus movement, some think that as long as they keep believing "their cars won't crash, they won't get cancer, and if they're drafted and sent to Vietnam 'we won't be killed or even scratched.'" (*Life,* May 14, 1971, p. 82) Although we believe in prayer, we know that God has not built a fence around His people so that none of them can be harmed as long as they believe. Paul, for example, had a thorn in the flesh and he and the other apostles died.

There are "healers" who tell people if they have faith enough they will be healed. This gives them the excuse, when a person is not healed, of blaming the failure on the individual and not on the healer who supposedly had received power. (Acts 1:8)

If we just have faith enough we can do anything is a wrong belief for three reasons. *First,* it is not scriptural. *Second,* it leads some people into agony for they blame all failures and sicknesses on their lack of faith and think that they are not qualified as Christians because they don't have this sort of miracle-working faith. *Third,* it leads some to deny Christ because, though they have faith enough to suffer and even die, the sought-for results fail to come.

Pentecostalism is also characterized by false doctrine, but which is not exposed by the so-called modern revelations. In fact, these conflicting doctrines are "confirmed" by their "signs" for those who teach these doctrines perform the same type of "wonders". The next chapter will deal with some cases.

Chapter III

False Doctrines and Contradictions

Pentecostalism is characterized by contradictions. There are contradictions not only between their claims and their works, but also in their teachings. They all perform the same type of signs, but they teach different doctrines. God is not the author of confusion and contradiction. When Moses and the magicians of Egypt got into a wonder-working contest, before it was over even Pharaoh knew who was on God's side. (Ex. 7:11, 22; 8:7, 18; 9:11; 12:29-36) When Elijah and the prophets of Baal got into a miracle-working contest it was clearly demonstrated who was on God's side. (1 Kings 18:20-40)

Members of different denominations, teaching different doctrines, claim the gifts; especially tongues. To give one illustration, Johannes Fabian has recently written a book on *Jama: A Charismatic Movement in Katanga* (Evanston, Illinois, 60201: Northwestern University Press, 1972) How can one movement be guided by the Spirit, when it rejects water baptism as a part of the new birth, and another movement be guided by the Spirit and accept baptism as a part of the new birth? It may be said that the Spirit will gradually lead these people to the same position. How could this be done, since each of them claims the guidance of the Spirit now and each has the same sort of signs? When the apostles were baptized in the Spirit on Pentecost, and people wanted to know what to do to be saved, it was not months or years before they learned. Instead, that very day the people were told to repent and to be baptized. (Acts 2:38) Although there were three days between the time Saul saw the Lord and he learned about baptism, he was quickly informed when a disciple of the Lord was placed in contact with him. Saul did not have peace spoken to him by Christ; instead, he had to learn from an earthen vessel — Ananias — what he must do. (Acts 9:6, 10-19) Shortly after he saw Saul, Ananias told him not to tarry, but to arise and be baptized and wash away his sins. (Acts 22:16) When Paul preached to the Corinthians, those who heard and believed were baptized. (Acts 18:8)

By transferring authority from the Bible to one's personal experience, there are those among us who conclude that though people, who have received similar "gifts" to what they have received, have not been baptized, yet they are viewed as having been forgiven. This contradicts Acts 2:38.

Although he thought they should be a part of "a local church so that they can have a spiritual home," Harald Bredesen said: "Well, I don't say that they have to be a member of any church because I'm not convinced that church membership is scriptural." (*Logos Journal*, Jan.-Feb. 1972, p. 25) Membership in a denominational church is not scriptural. Membership in Christ's church is not like membership in a lodge. However, if we are in Christ we are members of, we are a part of, His body the church. (Eph. 1:22-23; 2:13-16) Even with reference to spiritual gifts, all members did not perform the same function; nor do they with reference to natural gifts. However, they are members of the same body — Christ's church. (1 Cor. 12:12-27)

DAVID WILKERSON

David Wilkerson, the author of *The Cross and the Switchblade,* which helped convert Pat Boone, thinks that some have gone "overboard" on tongues. He said some "preach tongues more than Christ," some say you cannot be saved without it, and that he did not believe the Spirit "makes a fool of anyone." To him "true Holy Ghost baptism is a 'baptism of love' that helps you see and love a lost world through the eyes of Jesus."

He also wrote: "I speak with tongues in my secret closet of prayer. It is a beautiful devotional experience with me. It is not a group or public experience. No one else is involved but Jesus and me!" (*David Wilkerson Speaks Out,* Brooklyn, N.Y. 11238, 444 Clinton Ave.: Teen Challenge Publications, June 1972, pp. 4-5)

Christians need to be filled with love. But if the baptism of the Spirit were love, everyone baptized in the Spirit would be immersed in love but Wilkerson indicates that all are not. The baptism of the Spirit involves the miraculous. Tongues were not for the purpose of private devotionals, but were a sign to confirm

FALSE DOCTRINES AND CONTRADICTIONS

the word. (Mk. 16:17-18, 20; Acts 1:1-4, 6, 8, 11; 1 Cor. 14:22) Why doesn't Wilkerson understand these things?

Wilkerson also said: "Pity the poor Catholic who speaks with tongues. His own church doesn't know how to react—old line Pentecostals insist they 'leave the harlot mother church' . . ." (p. 5) How could it be that the Spirit would leave them in Roman Catholicism instead of leading them into the church which is the body of Christ?

He also wrote: "For the past five years I have refused to speak for the Full Gospel Businessmen. I disagreed with their view of the baptism of the Holy Ghost. It seemed to me they were always pointing to their banner, which read, 'Our Banner Is Love,' while putting down denominations and solid organizations. Businessmen seemed to be saying, 'Last year I only made $20,000—but I received the Holy Ghost and now I make $50,000 a year.' To me, it appeared to be a special 'in group' who traveled the world over to swap stories about deliverances from denominational ties—about financial successes—and prize 'catches' for the baptism God had given them. But I see now a prejudice in my own heart just as grievous as that of critics who fight them on doctrinal grounds. In spite of their stumbling—in spite of their excesses—God is using them. I want to rejoice with them." (*David Wilkerson Speaks Out,* June 1972, p. 6)

We do not want to leave the impression that he is against tongues, but he was appealing for more love. We agree that more love is needed, but it is a moral or spiritual fruit of the Spirit, which comes through following Christ, and not a miraculous gift.

Although we differ with Mr. Wilkerson on the gifts and some other matters, one cannot differ with his desire to help young people, and the fact that he has reached drug addicts. Our faith is not a living faith if we just argue against false doctrine but do not try to help people to know Christ, to help them with their problems, and to try to get them to walk in faith and love based on Christ and His word.

CONTRADICT

Why do the gifts sometimes contradict the scriptures, even according to the admission of at least some of them? Harald Bredesen spoke of some in the Pentecostal movement who were "always looking for some new thing. The danger I see is that some charismatic churches have to have a revelation a day. One pastor said, 'You know my people are afraid to go on vacation for fear they'll miss the latest revelation.'" He said he saw "this over and over." They usually thought if you were "not in their group then you've missed God's best. It gets to be a real spiritual tyranny, governed by the gifts."

"My advice to the individuals in it who are being terrorized by spiritual leaders is to look to God. Get alone and let his Spirit speak to you. His messages do not always have to come from the gifts but rather from the Bible and his word speaking to your heart. I would remind the leaders that all interpretations and words of wisdom are subject to the error of men and must be checked against the Scriptures." ("Life in the Spirit," *Logos Journal,* Jan.-Feb., 1972, p. 24)

How can these interpretations, if given by men guided by the Spirit, be wrong? How could the words of wisdom, if one has the gift of wisdom from the Spirit, contradict the Spirit in the Scriptures? A gift would be of no value, but very dangerous, if it leads one contrary to the Bible. I wonder whether or not Pat Boone has been able yet to get Bredesen, who helped convert Pat to Pentecostalism, to check with the Scriptures on the subject of water baptism? Bredesen left the Reformed Church, and now is "pastoring an independent Jesus People Church" which he calls "a real New Testament church (Trinity Christian Center, Vancouver, B.C.)". (Harald Bredesen, with Pat King, "Life in the Spirit." *Logos Journal,* Jan.-Feb. 1972, p. 25)

The extent to which any of these people get together is not based on modern revelations and gifts but on the extent to which they are willing to listen, accept and obey what is taught in the Bible.

There are some among us who teach that we should have living apostles of Christ today, while there are others with similar "gifts" who deny it. One thought that the twelve had a special place (Matt. 19:28), but he said: I "believe that apostles are still with us giving the Holy Spirit as in Acts 8. . . ." But who among us has the qualifications of apostles of Christ? I have discussed this subject in detail in *Apostles or Apostates?* When asked to name someone today who was an apostle of Christ, one person named some people who would deny that they are apostles. Another wrote: "An apostle is one who does the work of an apostle — one who allows himself to be used of God to deliver one who would be born of God." An apostle could do this (1 Cor. 4:15), but so can others through the gospel. This person claimed to have some gifts. Why didn't he know the qualifications of an apostle of Christ?

There are some who claim that there are modern revelations

FALSE DOCTRINES AND CONTRADICTIONS

which should be a part of the Bible, and there are others who deny it.

MODERN REVELATIONS

The miracles in the Bible were used to start things. For example, the miracles of the creation of man and of woman. The human race was perpetuated by natural law. Miracles were involved in the revelation and confirmation of God's message. *The revelation and the confirmation went hand in hand.* (Mk. 16:17-18, 20; Heb. 2:3-4) If we have confirmers today, we must have revealers today. The inspired men mentioned in Hebrews 2:3-4, did not work miracles to prove that Moses was inspired of God but to prove they were inspired of God. If we have confirmers today, they should confirm the word which they are preaching and not the word of someone centuries ago. Of course, it would help prove Paul was inspired of God if they are inspired today and teach us that Paul also was inspired. However, it would do so only because their miracles had proved that *they* today are inspired messengers of God.

One among us said that "Acts 28 is open ended. Where tablets of human hearts are available to Him, God through His Christ and His Spirit is still writing scriptures. Through His gifts these messages find ears eager to hear what the Spirit is saying to the churches." He also claimed that in contending with Pat Boone, Warren Lewis, and with him that I was not contending with them but "with the Holy Spirit himself for the minds of men. Anyone who is spiritual in the sense that Paul used the term in 1 Cor. 14:37 or anyone who claims to be a prophet has either had no problem or expressed no problem with the things I have written." The last time I questioned Pat Boone on the subject he disclaimed inspiration, and he did not think that people today are writing scriptures which should be accepted and quoted as authoritative along with the Bible.

IF WE HAVE ENOUGH FAITH?

One wrote: "Whenever men look with confidence to the Lord *signs will follow belief.*" "According to John, Jesus made some specific statements about what *a person who believed in him* could expect." *First,* "He said that *the one who believed* in him would do the works that he did." However, this individual does not raise the dead or walk on the water, although he lives close to the Atlantic Ocean. Jesus also said they would do *greater* works. Does he do greater miracles than Christ? We have already dealt with this, but let us repeat it.

Christ was speaking to the apostles. (John 13; Matt. 25:20-26) He called on them to believe, and promised they would do the works which He had done and even greater works. (John 14:9-22) Since they did not do greater miracles, Jesus must have had in mind some other type of works. They were to do the greater works because He went to the Father. (John 14:12) He went to the Father and sent the Spirit who enabled them to do the greater works. They did greater works: (1) Geographically. (2) Nationally and racially. (Eph. 2:13-19) (3) Christ taught the gospel in promise, and they taught it in fulfillment. (4) Numerically. (5) Duration in time. (6) Christ taught that His reign was at hand (Matt. 4:17, 23), but they proclaimed Him as reigning. (Acts 2:34-36; Col. 1:13) Of course, their work was really His work through them.

Second, the same person wrote that to each believer the Spirit is promised as his Counselor, and "that this Counselor would teach the believer all things." If this applies to him, he should have an inspired recollection of what Jesus taught, and should be guided directly (not through the New Testament) into all the truth. (John 14:26; 16:12-15) However, he does not know anything about the inspired word of God except what he has learned from the Bible, or from someone who learned it from the Bible.

Third, he applied Mk. 16:17-18 to himself, but does he cast out demons, speak with new tongues or languages (Mk. 16:20; Acts 2:4, 6, 8, 11), take up serpents, not hurt by any deadly thing he drinks, and does he lay hands on the sick and they recover without any failures?

Fourth, he applied Acts 1:8 to himself, so this means that he and all true believers have the power which the apostles had. Unless he can do all these things on his own logic he is not a believer.

One of them wrote that unless we have the baptism of the Spirit in a miraculous way, we remain in the womb and are content with the water. If this is true, one has not been born into the kingdom unless he has the miraculous manifestations. For Jesus spoke of *one* birth which involved water and Spirit. (John 3:3-5) There are other Pentecostals among us that will say that one can be in the kingdom even if he does not have the miraculous manifestations.

The Samaritans had become Christians, and therefore they must have undergone the new birth. However, it was not until later that they received miraculous power through the laying on of the apostles' hands. (Acts 8:12, 14-18) Therefore, the miraculous was not in itself a part of the new birth.

One very sincere young man told me he had a small gift of healing. If the person had something very seriously wrong with him, he was not able to do anything since his gift was small.

He also misunderstood the baptism of the Holy Spirit and thought that it was being filled with love. All cases of the baptism of the Spirit involved the miraculous. (Acts 1:5, 8; 2:1-4, 6, 8, 11, 33; Acts 10:44-48)

SIGNS TO PRODUCE FAITH

Some maintain that the signs were not designed to produce faith, but *to follow* faith. Of those who ask for signs to produce faith, one said that "Jesus gave his pronouncement . . . 'An evil and adulterous generation seeks for a sign, but no other sign will be given.'" *First,* since he thinks he is inspired, does he think the Spirit led him to stop quoting where he did and thereby distort the passage? Jesus did not say: "but no other sign will be given." He said: "and there shall no sign be given to it *but the sign of Jonah the prophet. . . .*" (Matt. 12:39) Will he give us today this sign of the death, burial, and resurrection? Or does he think this sign was given once for all? Since he applied this passage to people today, who ask for signs to produce faith, why doesn't he give this generation this sign?

Second, the word of God makes clear that the miracles were designed to produce faith. (Mk. 16:20; Acts 2:22; John 20:30-31; Heb. 2:3-4) Of course, they would not produce faith if a person's heart was set against God's will.

Third, the people in Matt. 12 had seen and acknowledged Christ's miracles. They realized that some of these miracles were directly against the devil and his agents. The reason they did not believe was not a lack of signs, for Jesus had wrought many signs, but a lack of a receptive heart. (Acts 2:22; Lk. 8:11-15) However, even this evil and adulterous generation (which was the reason they were not receptive to the signs) was given the sign of the prophet Jonah. (Matt. 12:39)

Fourth, I am not a sign seeker, for I am satisfied with the signs recorded in the Bible. Men who say that we must have the signs today are the sign seekers. When we ask them to do — to work the signs — what *they* say one must do in order to truly believe, they have no right to view us as the sign seekers and apply this passage to us. We are simply asking them to *demonstrate,* what they say believers can and must do, *or desist* from such claims.

If these people had the gifts, they would know the purposes of the miracles. Furthermore, they would demonstrate their miraculous power to furnish reasons for unbelievers to become believers.

WOMEN PREACHERS

How can a group of people be guided by the Spirit and yet contradict the Spirit without being rebuked by their inspired teachers? Women preachers are common among Pentecostals. Concerning the work of women, we observe briefly: *First,* there is much that she can do, and she needs to emphasize what she can do and not what she cannot do. (Acts 9:36, 39; 18:26; Titus 2:3-5, etc.)

Second, she has the spiritual privileges of being a child of God and an heir. There is no difference between male and female concerning these matters. (Gal. 3:26-29) However, Paul did not mean that we are neuter gender, for a woman was still a woman and a man was still a man; a slave was still a slave and a free man was still free.

Third, women were not apostles, evangelists, public preachers nor did they lead prayers in the presence of the men. (1) Someone may say that Paul did not condemn women preaching or praying in the assembly but only the manner in which they were doing it. (1 Cor. 11:2-16) However, they overlook the fact that Paul later said they were not to do it at all. (1 Cor. 14:33-35) The word for "keep silence" meant — among other things — they were not to make a speech. (compare 14:28, 30) Paul first condemned the *manner* in which they were doing it, and *then* the very *doing* of it. Sometimes Paul deals with a problem on more than one ground. For example, in the same letter he first condemned eating meat in an idol's temple as a violation of the law of love; even if an idol was nothing. (1 Cor. 8) Later in the same epistle he said it was wrong within itself. (1 Cor. 10:14-22) (2) In a mixed assembly of men and women Paul showed that men were to lead prayer. He used the word for men as distinguished from women, and the context also shows the same thing. Paul included every place, so whether it was the Lord's assembly or some other mixed assembly, the men were to lead in prayer. (1 Tim. 2:8-15) Of course, women can pray silently any time, and can follow in their hearts the one who leads the prayer in an assembly.

How strange it is that some "spirit" leads many Pentecostals today to ignore what the Spirit said through Paul. Paul rebuked such. (1 Cor. 14:37)

FALSE DOCTRINES AND CONTRADICTIONS

GLORIFY CHRIST

Jesus said that the Spirit "shall glorify me: for he shall take of mine, and shall declare it unto you." (John 16:14) The Spirit came to make us conscious of Christ and not especially conscious of the Spirit. He came to show to us the things of Christ. He came to glorify Jesus. When we read, beginning with Acts 2, how the Spirit fulfilled this promise of Christ we see that through Acts, the epistles, and Revelation the emphasis is on Jesus Christ and what He has done, and does, for us. We accept all that is taught in the Bible concerning the Spirit, insofar as we understand it, but we must never forget that the Spirit did not come to glorify Himself but to glorify Christ.

In the thinking and writing of some, baptism into Christ — with all that it means according to the Bible — fades into insignificance in comparison with what they call the baptism in the Spirit. Somehow or another this is viewed as far superior to baptism into Christ.

PREMILLENNIAL

There are some of the Pentecostals who are premillennial and some who are not. In personal correspondence Pat Boone has said he does not know when Jesus is coming, and that the important thing is to be ready — which is true. However, there are published statements of the following nature. In an article Tom Shales said that Pat thinks that "the Jesus movement is a great last minute effort . . . but 'it won't change the destiny of man.'

"That destiny includes the end of the world in from 10 to 15 years, following the establishment of a one-world dictatorship piloted by an anti-Christ — maybe Chairman Mao, he speculates. Then the oceans will turn to one-third blood and the earth may shift on its axis. Earthquakes are early evidence of this." ("Pat Boone and Family," *The Washington Post,* May 15, 1972, p. B2)

In a magazine, *Jesus Christ-Solid Rock* (published at 13645 Beta Rd., Dallas, Texas. No date on the article), there is an article by Pat entitled "I Have a Hope." He wrote: "The Jesus movement among our young was prophesied long ago in God's word . . . now God is fulfilling prophecy and pouring out His Spirit upon our youth.

"The miracle of God's Spirit is being experienced in every area of society I know. My business acquaintances, actor and actress associates, laymen and minister friends — so many of them are finding a new dimension in the Holy Spirit. Long ago, God's Word said this would occur in the last days."

"I believe Jesus Christ is coming back for His people very soon!

"The fascinating truth is that this event is destined to be experienced by my generation."

However, the last days started on Pentecost around 2,000 years ago. Peter said that this was that which was spoken of by the prophet Joel. (Acts 2:16-17. Compare Heb. 1:1) We have devoted an entire chapter to this in *The Hub of the Bible*.

Pat went on to say that today we have seen Israel rebuilt in the face of her enemies, and that: "Jesus warned that we who have watched the rebuilding of the Israeli nation are a *destined generation*. We should know, as positively as spring buds announce the summer, that the season has come: the end He spoke of is near!" Pat then quoted Lk. 21:31-32. He thinks that "this generation" is the one living today. Also that: "Ezekiel prophesied the Moscovites' hatred of Israel centuries ago." (pp. 22-23) Although we do not have space to go into a discussion here, we believe that the kingdom which Jesus spoke of as being at hand was the one which was at hand in the first century. (Matt. 3:2; 4:17, 23; 10:7; Mk. 9:1), and which was proclaimed to men on the first Pentecost after Christ's resurrection. M. Kik has a good book entitled *Matthew 24* which covers the same events mentioned in Luke 21. In my book, *The Kingdom: Prophesied and Established,* it is shown that the kingdom prophesied by the prophets, is the present kingdom of Christ. (Psa. 110:1-4; Acts 2:34-36; Col. 1:13; Heb. 8:1-4) Certain aspects of this have also been discussed in a book which we hope to publish shortly, God willing, on *Prophecy and Premillennialism*. Christ's present reign continues until the last enemy, death, is conquered. This is at His second coming, and it brings the end of the world and the entrance into eternal glory, and not the establishment of His kingdom on this earth. (Acts 2:34-35; 1 Cor. 15:24-28; Rev. 20:11-21:5)

I do not know all of Pat's ideas about the kingdom, but he is confused in thinking that the last days started with this generation, or that the second coming brings the kingdom to earth.

These are but samples of false and contradictory teachings which are found in modern Pentecostalism.

Chapter IV

The Sufficiency of Scriptures

A basic issue involved in Pentecostalism is whether the Scriptures are sufficient and final. As we have pointed out, if we have the gifts today they should be for the same fundamental purpose for which they were given in the first century; that is to reveal and confirm truth. (Heb. 2:3-4) If we have inspired men today, we have more revelations from God. When these men write, we have more scriptures. The Mormons are consistent and maintain that there are new scriptures.

INSPIRED?

Some claim inspiration and new inspired writings. When I asked one brother whether he was inspired, he wrote: "Frankly, I had never given it a thought until you brought up the matter." This shows that he was ignorant of the nature and function of the gifts, and therefore did not have any of the gifts. Imagine Paul saying that about his writings! (I Cor. 14:37) He went on to say: "I have the same Spirit as did Paul, Peter, John and Jesus in the same way that they did — the difference — they according to their call, their faith, their confidence in God and their willingness to be used by Him according to His purposes." "I believe that God through his Spirit works in lives today as in the first century and that a record of such working is as much part of the history of the church as that recorded by Luke." There are others with the same so-called gifts, and guided supposedly by the same Spirit, who do not agree with him.

WRITTEN WORD MINIMIZED

This same person minimized the written word. He thought that some of us have the word, but not what it promises. We read the cook book but do not eat the meal. "If reading the Bible satisfies your appetite, rather than whet it, it is because you have never tasted that the Lord is good. Your filter has caused you to settle for the book rather than enjoy the feast it describes."

First, the word promised me remission of sins, sonship in Christ, and the hope of life eternal. Believing God, and submitting to His will in becoming and remaining a Christian, I enjoy the word and such wonderful promises. He himself wrote, in the very next paragraph, "Where man determines to know nothing except Jesus Christ and Him crucified; he reigns in life, through Christ." The miracles were to reveal and confirm the gospel that we may be saved through the gospel. (1 Cor. 15:1-5) Having salvation in Christ is having what the word promised, among other things which it promises, and this surpasses the miraculous gifts.

Second, the word of God itself is food — both milk and meat, although due to their immaturity Paul was feeding the Corinthians milk. (1 Cor. 3:2) "How sweet are thy words unto my taste! Yea, sweeter than honey to my mouth!" (Psa. 119:103) Of course, we must not only read, but believe in and walk by the word of God. Does he think that because one does not have the gifts that he has never tasted that the Lord is good?

He also minimized the written word when he wrote me that: "The written word alone avails little, and confirms nothing. The written word quickened by God's Holy Spirit becomes the living word which ushers the believer into the spiritual realms — There is no other access!" To this we reply: *First,* although he did not spell out in this statement what he means by the word being quickened by the Spirit, what he has said about the Spirit and the believer indicates that he means a quickening in some miraculous way such as the presence of the gifts or by direct inspiration. *Second,* since the word of God, whether written or spoken, is the seed of the kingdom the word is never alone in the sense of being without quickening power. There is life in the seed for it is God's word. (Heb. 4:12) Of course, it cannot bring forth fruit in hearts which are wayside soil. (Lk. 8:11-15) *Third,* even when read by enemies of Christ, the written word is the voice of God speaking to them even if they refuse to listen. (Matt. 22:31-32) The written word is the voice of the Spirit (Rev. 2:1, 7), the witness of the Spirit (Heb. 10:15-17), to reject the word spoken by an inspired man was to refuse to listen to the Spirit (Acts 7:51-53; Neh. 9:30), it is the voice of the prophets (Acts 13:27), and to have their word is to have the prophet in the sense that we can listen to them. (Lk. 16:29-31) The written word can produce faith (John 20:30-31; Lk. 8:12; Rom. 10:17), certainty (Lk. 1:3, 4), understanding (Eph. 3:4), regulate conduct (1 Tim. 3:14-15), convey commandments (1 Cor. 14:37), warn us (1 Cor. 4:14), guard us against error (2 Tim. 3:13-15), stir us up (2 Pet. 1:12-13), exhort us (1 Pet. 5:12), and make our joy full. (1 John 1:4) It is profitable for teaching, reproof, correction, and instruction in righteousness. It can make us wise unto salvation and furnish us completely unto every good work. (2 Tim. 3:16-17) How can a man, who claims to be anointed with a miraculous reception of the Spirit, take such a dim view of God's written word? Is not our attitude toward His word an essential part of our attitude toward Him?

BRINGING THE BIBLE DOWN TO MAN'S LEVEL

Warren Lewis, who advocates the miraculous gifts today, brings the Bible down to man's level by claiming that the writers of the Gospels contradict one another. He said in such cases they cannot both be right and "they might both be wrong." There are clashing and jarring things in the Gospels which cannot be reconciled with one another. "No one point—great or small—is so important that it cannot be questioned or gainsaid or weighted another way. Even truth about Jesus Christ in one Gospel can be turned around in another Gospel." (*Mission,* Jan. 1972, pp. 3, 6, 9) He concluded that we could never use the Bible as a weapon against another, that it was not a "blueprint" for "building a church or a 'text book' for doctrine or a 'road map' from earth to heaven." "Scripture is not 'absolute,' 'inerrant,' 'infallible,' or 'perfect.' " (p. 9) This was the only article in the issue which the editor of *Mission* singled out for special endorsement as an honest effort to speak where the Bible speaks. (p. 30) It is clear that: (1) Many of the Pentecostals among us will not endorse this view of the Bible. (2) It contradicts Paul's statement that the word of God is the sword of the Spirit; for what is a sword to be used for if not in combat in contending for the faith. (Eph. 6:17; Jude 3) (3) He contradicted himself for he tried to use the Bible against us and our position concerning the gifts and concerning its inspiration.

Another brother, when I pointed out contradictions in Pentecostalism, said that Peter made a mistake. Peter's mistake was not in teaching a doctrine which contradicted some teaching of another inspired man, but in his failure to live up to the doctrine which he himself had taught, by the Spirit, concerning the Gentiles. Therefore, Paul rebuked him for not walking upright according to the truth of the Gospel. (Acts 15:7-11; Gal. 2:14)

The inspired men were guided into truth, not error. (John 16:12-15; 17:8, 17, 20-21; Matt. 28:20; Acts 2:42; 1 Cor. 14:37; 2 Thess. 2:13-15)

SEEKING SIGNS RATHER THAN SCRIPTURES

Another manifestation of the undermining of the authority and sufficiency of the Bible is found in the fact that some follow what they interpret as present day signs from God rather than what God has revealed in His word.

The faith has once for all been delivered unto the saints, and it makes all the difference in the world whether we look for a sign or for a scripture. (Jude 3) Do we know God's will through searching the Scriptures and through studiously and prayerfully applying his word to life, or do we learn His will through some sign which we ask for and decide that we have found?

A leader in a congregation abandoned his wife and children, a woman abandoned her husband and children, and they thought they loved one another. They knew it was God's will, because they had asked for and received a sign. How many times they asked for a sign before they got the go-ahead we do not know. If they had been searching the Scriptures rather than hunting for signs, they could easily have found some which spoke of not coveting one's neighbor's wife and of being faithful to one's own wife and family.

When God was sending inspired prophets into the world, and confirming their work with miraculous signs (Heb. 1:1-2; 2:1-4), those who claimed to be prophets had to pass more than one test. In the Old Testament two of the tests were their teaching and whether or not their signs came to pass. If the sign the person gave failed, he was a false prophet. (Deut. 18:20-22) However, if a successful sign was given, and the prophet led them after false gods, they were to reject the prophet. (Deut. 13:1-5) A true prophet would not teach contrary to God's word.

The New Testament teaches that some claimed to do miracles but were rejected because they had not done God's will. (Matt. 7:21) There are lying wonders which help lead some to accept strong delusions. (2 Thess. 2:10-12)

The heart is deceitful above all things (Jer. 17:9), and this is why all must be measured by God's word. When one set up an idol in his heart in the Old Testament, God answered him according to the multitude of his idols. (Ezek. 14:1-5) God's word is truth (John 17:17), and those who do not love the truth and take pleasure in unrighteousness will receive strong delusions. (2 Thess. 2:10-12; 2 Tim. 4:3-4) God will bring evil on them, even the fruit of their own thoughts. "Hear, O earth: behold, I will bring evil upon this people, even the fruit of their thoughts, because they have not hearkened unto my words; and as for my law, they have rejected it." (Jer. 6:19)

People who seek for signs rather than for scriptures, and the intelligent use of their mind (for we are to love God with all of our mind also) in applying the Scriptures, are people who will end up walking according to the desires of their own hearts rather than by the will of God. And is it not instructive that those who seek "signs" and "wonders" today get the same sort of "signs" and "wonders" but they teach conflicting doctrines? None of them do what the apostles and prophets did in the New Testament, and sooner or later all of them contradict the truth, the faith into which the inspired apostles and prophets were guided in the first century. (John 16:12-15; Jude 3; Heb. 2:3-4)

The unreliability of subjective experience can be illustrated by the following quotation. "The setting sun painted the horizon in psychedelic hues as Muriel Tepper-Dorner, a channel for the

THE SUFFICIENCY OF SCRIPTURES

White Brotherhood, demonstrated the light-radiation way to salvation. 'Breathe in the golden light, and see yourself as a sun,' she instructed. 'Radiate the light out to each other until we see this whole room filled with light. Now radiate more light, and see it flowing all over this campus, and now all over the planet.'

"A freshman co-ed, absorbed in it all, turned to her date and whispered, 'I swear I can feel it coming out of my skin. I have to be careful, or I'll get drained.'" (Richard W. Coffen, "Is Instant Salvation the Real Thing?", *These Times,* August, 1972, p. 3. Nashville, Tenn. 37202: Southern Publishing Co., P. O. Box 59.)

Our emotions, impulses, and our interpretation of so-called signs today are not dependable foundations. They are the least dependable things about us for so many things affect our emotions, and we can keep asking for some sort of sign until we get something we interpret as the sign which says for us to go ahead or not go ahead as the case may be.

AUTHORITY OF BIBLE UNDERMINED

Do not these things make clear that Pentecostalism, when carried to its logical conclusions, undermines the sufficiency and finality of the Bible? *First,* its stress on personal experience, when followed consistently, places the authority of the experience over the Bible. Their gifts and signs prove they have the right doctrine, they think. It is true that Christianity must be experienced. It is the life which is directed by Christ's teaching. (Titus 2:11-14) We experience the new birth by actually being born of water and the Spirit, and we experience the new life in Christ by living it. However, our experiences must be based on, regulated by, and be in subjection to the word of God.

Second, the finality of the Bible is undermined, because if men are inspired today we have additional revelations and need not confine ourselves to the faith once for all delivered in the first century. (Jude 3)

Third, the written word is minimized by many of them.

Fourth, with many of them the gifts overshadow the teaching. The miraculous gifts in the Bible were given in order to reveal and confirm the truth of God. The gifts were a means to an end, and not an end within themselves. The signs of Mark 16:17-18 were designed to confirm the word which the sign workers taught. (Mk. 16:20) The Spirit came on Pentecost to enable the apostles to reveal and confirm the truths which they preached. The miracles of Jesus accredited Him as a teacher sent from God. (John 3:1-2; Acts 2:22) The gifts were to bear witness to those who were delivering the great salvation. (Heb. 2:3-4) Tongues were not to be used unless they reached the understanding of the audience and built them up through instruction and exhortation. (1 Cor. 14)

How different are the so-called gifts today! There are some individuals who study the teaching of the Bible, yield themselves to God, and even try to live holy lives as *means* through which they can get the gifts. We are not saying that this is true of all of them. However, all of them with whom the author has had contact have in fact, although sometimes they have denied it because they did not realize what they were doing, elevated the gifts over the teaching. This is clear from their contention that various denominationalists who repudiate some things in the Bible, which those among us accept as the teaching of the Bible, have the same gifts which these brethren have. That denominationalists have the gifts is therefore viewed as being more important than whether they have been born of water and the Spirit, whether they contend for the faith once for all delivered to the saints, and whether they accept the one church which is Christ's body.

LUTHER'S STATEMENT

Martin Luther recognized that when one sought the word of the Spirit in a subjective experience that he was adrift. He wrote that the Spirit does not separate Himself "from the spoken Word" but that He leads us "into all truth through it . . . far too often experience has taught me that when the devil catches me outside of Scripture, when I begin to roam around with my thoughts and flutter heavenward, he brings me to the point where I do not know what is to become of God or of me. Christ, therefore, wants this truth . . . so tied down that we put aside reason and all our own ideas and feelings and simply cling to the Word, considering it the one truth." (Ewald Plass, *What Luther Says,* St. Louis: Concordia Publishing House, 1959, Vol. II, p. 664. Quoted by Vernon Harley, "Pentecost and the Charismatic Movement," *The Christian News,* June 26, 1972, p. 7)

PRAYER AND PROVIDENCE

The sufficiency and finality of the Bible, the fact that we do not have miraculous power, does not mean that we are not to pray.

There is a vast difference between our having supernatural power which enables us to tell someone to walk in the name of Jesus of Nazareth (Acts 1:8; 3:6-10, 16; 4:9-10), and our praying for the sick. *First,* we pray for our daily bread, but we also work without expecting manna from heaven or the multiplication of loaves and fishes. (Ex. 16:15, 35; Matt. 6:11; John 6:5-14, 31; Eph. 4:28; 2 Thess. 3:10-14) A miracle was a supernatural, superhuman work done by God through inspired men in order to confirm their

THE SUFFICIENCY OF SCRIPTURES

message. God is not so limited that He cannot answer prayer without working a miracle. He can work behind the scenes in His providence and, without any supernatural manifestation, answer prayer. David prayed that God would turn the counsel of Ahithophel into foolishness. David then did what he could. God overruled and answered the prayer, but there was no supernatural sign. He did it, but we do not know exactly how. (2 Sam. 15:31; 32-34; 16:23; 17:7, 14) God carried out His promise to protect Saul in Corinth, but there was no supernatural manifestation, as there was in the deliverance of Peter. (Acts 18:9-10, 12-17; 12:7-11)

Second, is not prayer supernatural, so that if God answers prayer in any way is it not a miraculous manifestation of God's power? (1) Our prayers are neither inspired nor supernatural manifestations. Our speaking to the Supernatural Being is not in itself supernatural. (2) If God answering our prayer, without working a miracle, is a supernatural answer, there is no distinction between the natural and the supernatural. In such a case everything is natural and everything is supernatural. How could there be any supernatural manifestations which were signs? As we have pointed out elsewhere, the miracles were supernatural events, which functioned as signs, and which could be seen even by the unbeliever. (3) There is surely a difference between God answering in a natural way a man's prayer for a wife, and God taking something from the side of man, fashioning him a wife, and presenting the wife to him when he awakes from the operation. (4) There is a difference between God overruling and keeping a person from drowning, without a visible display of supernatural power, and enabling one to walk on the water.

If this movement (Pentecostalism) was miraculously taught by the Spirit, these people would know the difference between our having power to work miracles, and our not having power but petitioning God in prayer. There is a difference between God working behind the scenes, overruling to bring about the answer to our prayers, and God making a visible, supernatural manifestation of power.

With reference to the miracles, there is no case — after the coming of the Spirit on Pentecost — when any inspired man tried to work a miracle and failed. However, prayer is not always answered in the affirmative. God may say, Yes; He may say, No; or He may say, Wait awhile.

EXPERIENCE NOT THE STANDARD

We are to be judged by Christ and His Word, which Word we can know only because God has revealed it. (John 12:48; Acts

17:30-31; 1 Cor. 2:10-13) Those who determine their spiritual standing by their subjective experience, instead of by the Word of God, are not measuring themselves by the standard by which they shall be judged. Jesus made it clear that some, who concluded they were right because they measured themselves by what they assumed they had done — and supposedly in the name of the Lord, were wrong because they had not done God's will. "Many will say to me in that day, Lord, Lord, did we not prophesy by thy name, and by thy name cast out demons, and by thy name do many mighty works? And then will I profess unto them, I never knew you: depart from me, ye that work iniquity." (Matt. 7:21-23) If they did not think they had done these things, surely they would not have brought them up to the Lord on judgment day. Jesus went on to say that we must both *hear* and *do* His word. (Matt. 7:24-27) They depended on their experience, and their interpretation of it, and failed to measure themselves by God's word.

There are individuals who do not love the truth but take pleasure in unrighteousness. They receive strong delusions. (2 Thess. 2:10-12) When they measure themselves by their subjective experiences they find them *strong,* but if they measured themselves by the Word of God they would realize that these were strong *delusions.*

When dealing with those who put their personal experience ahead of the Bible, as the authority in religion, ask them how they can know that Matt. 7:21-23, (or 2 Thess. 2:10-12) does not describe them unless they measure themselves by God's Word? One may lead some of them to reconsider, but there are others who will "know" what they feel in their hearts and what the Bible says will not move them. One may make the additional appeal that they would not know there was the Holy Spirit unless the Bible had revealed it. Therefore, they ought to let the Bible also settle the matter as to what the Spirit teaches.

When we say that experience is not the standard by which to determine whether we are doing God's will, we are not minimizing living the new life in Christ. There are reasons to eat the pudding, and there is a proof of the pudding in the eating thereof. Christ's teachings must be lived. (Lk. 6:46) If we just verbalize, our faith is dead. (Jas. 2:14-26) A vital test of our knowledge is whether we do the will of God. (1 John 2:3-4) We cannot separate knowing God from doing God's will. Through faith, knowledge of God's will, and living the new life we grow in grace and knowledge of the Lord. However, our experience must be directed by, and judged by, the word of God.

Chapter V

The Gifts Have Ceased

When we understand the purpose of the gifts we shall understand their duration. What are some of the things which show that the gifts have fulfilled their functions and have ceased?

THE FAILURE TO DEMONSTRATE

The fact that the gifts have ceased is demonstrated by the fact that they are not present today. *First,* who can demonstrate that their group possesses all of the gifts? Who has actual apostles of Jesus Christ today, with their authority, inspiration, and powers? *Second,* who today exercises the wide variety of gifts? *Third,* who has the wide variety of healing miracles? *Fourth,* whose healing "miracles" have the characteristics of the healing miracles of the Bible? Who never fails any time they attempt to work a miracle? *Fifth,* who has modern inspired scriptures which can hold up under examination? *Sixth,* since people with the same gifts teach contrary doctrines, who among them so clearly outshines the other that it is clear to see who has miraculous gifts from God? Where are the Moseses or the Elijahs among them who so clearly outshine the others that it is obvious who is on God's side?

Paul said that the miracles would cease. (1 Cor. 13:8-13) Some say they only ceased temporarily because of apostasy, but Paul said they would cease when that which was perfect or complete was come. They have ceased, so that which is perfect must have come. Paul was not speaking of Christ or the end of the world, but of the complete revelation in contrast with the incomplete. This passage is discussed in detail in *Pat Boone and the Gift of Tongues.*

THE MEANS HAVE CEASED

The means of obtaining the power have ceased. The only two cases mentioned in the Bible where miracles were manifested, apart from the laying on of the hands of the apostles of Christ, were the apostles themselves on Pentecost, and the household of Cornelius. The apostles were baptized in the Spirit by Christ directly from heaven. So was Cornelius. (Acts 1:5, 8; 2:1-4; 10:44-

48) The baptism of the apostles in the Spirit was to equip them to do the work which Christ wanted them to do. (John 14:26; 16:12-15) The baptism of Cornelius in the Spirit was to prove the point that God wanted proved, i.e., that the Gentiles were to receive the gospel without being bound by the law. Peter expressly said that it was God's way of bearing the Gentiles witness that they were not to be bound by the law but to be saved through the gospel. (Acts 15:7-11) He used it three times to prove this point: (1) At the household of Cornelius. (Acts 10:44-48) (2) In Jerusalem after he returned. (Acts 11:1-18) (3) In Jerusalem, when the matter of the Gentiles and the law was discussed. (Acts 15:7-11) No such case ever took place again. Why? Because God once and for all now had made the matter crystal clear.

All other cases of the reception of miraculous gifts was through the laying on of the hands of the apostles of Jesus Christ. Before the apostles laid hands on the seven, in Acts 6:6, 8; 8:6-7, there is no record of anyone besides the apostles working miracles.

Furthermore, although Philip worked miracles, he did not convey the Spirit in a miraculous way. The apostles did. Power must have been conferred because Simon saw that something had taken place, and he wanted the power to do what the apostles did. (Acts 8:11-19) If nothing happened when the apostles laid on hands, Simon already had "power" to lay on hands without anything happening.

The apostle Paul laid hands on certain disciples in Ephesus and they spoke in tongues. (Acts 19:1-6) He wanted to see the Romans and to confer some gift on them. (Rom. 1:11) If it could have been done simply through prayer, why did not Paul do it that way? Timothy received the gift through the laying on of Paul's hands (2 Tim. 1:6) It was with — accompanied by, but not through —.the hands of elders. (1 Tim. 4:14) However, it was *"through* the laying on of my hands," Paul said. (2 Tim. 1:6) Their hands must have accompanied Paul's hands, and they showed their approval, and they may have helped set Timothy apart for a special work; but the gift was actually given through Paul's hands. We have discussed the question, of the apostles' hands being the means through which the gifts were conferred, in *The Holy Spirit and the Christian,* as well as *Miracles or Mirages?* and the book concerning Pat Boone.

We have no apostles of Christ today, so we do not have the means of conferring the gifts.

There are people who seem to convey electricity, and so we have heard people say that when they had hands laid on them, and they received the Spirit, it was just like electricity going

THE GIFTS HAVE CEASED

through them. Where is any such indication that this was the way people in the first century knew they had received the Spirit in a miraculous way? They knew because the apostles had the power to confer the gifts, and they knew because they then had actual power to do something supernatural.

THE PURPOSES OF THE GIFTS HAVE BEEN FULFILLED

Who can show that the gifts are for us today but for different purposes than in the New Testament? The two basic purposes of miracles were to start things, and to reveal and confirm the truth.

God's way has been to start things by miracles and to perpetuate them by laws. God created the first man and woman by miracles. He did not say, in so many words, that He would not create other men and women. He did not say that He would never again create a man's wife from that which was taken from the side of man. However, the author would not advise anyone who is seeking for a wife to pray and expect God to bring him one as He did Adam. We know that God is not creating men and women as He did Adam and Eve, and we know that He set up the law of procreation in order to perpetuate the human race which had been started by miracles. Miracles were essential to the creation of the church and the revelation and confirmation of the gospel, but now that the word has been revealed the truth and the church are perpetuated through the spiritual seed line. (Eph. 1:19-23; Heb. 2:3-4; Lk. 8:11; Jude 3) The word today when obeyed produces Christians just as it did in the first century.

The miracles were designed to reveal and confirm the truth. (Heb. 2:3-4; 1 Cor. 14:26) If we must have confirmers today we must have revealers today. The revelation and the confirmation went hand in hand. Paul did not work miracles to prove that Moses was a prophet of God, but to prove that he, Paul, was a prophet of God. If someone today works miracles it should be to prove that he is an inspired messenger of God. Furthermore, he should reveal truths in addition to those revealed in the first century. Paul did not work miracles to confirm the word given centuries before but to confirm the word which was then being given through him. Modern miracle workers should be confirming new revelations, as well as have inspired remembrances of the New Testament, which are being delivered through them. At least some of them should write new scriptures. There is nothing in the scriptures which teaches that the gifts are to continue but that their basic purpose — the revelation and confirmation of truth — no longer functions. If the gifts are here today they are here for the same purposes for which they were given in the first century. Passages which speak of the gifts in several places also speak of their purposes. Just as the sacrifice of Christ was once for all, the faith was delivered once for all by the inspired men in the first century. (Heb. 7:27; Jude 3) We no more need new apostles and prophets each generation — for they are in the foundation — than we need a new Christ each generation. (Eph. 2:20) The gifts have ceased, for their purpose has been fulfilled. They revealed and confirmed the faith in the first century. They were means which ceased when they fulfilled their purpose, just as the scaffolding is removed after the building has been completed.

TESTED BY TEACHING

If these people have miraculous power, why the following: *First,* they do the same type of signs but contradict one another in their teaching. There are even pagan healers who can match them. *Second,* they contradict, sooner or later, the New Testament. Teaching, as well as claims, must be considered. (Deut. 13:1-5; 18:20-22; Matt. 7:21; 2 Thess. 2:10-12)

Those who claim the power are the ones who are obligated to demonstrate it, to have all the gifts, to write new scriptures, and to have the means of transmitting the gifts. They should have apostles who actually confer gifts.

Although I have heard of some amazing things, so far I have never seen them. And those I have seen were quite different when I read the write-up of them!

Since the faith has been once for all delivered to the saints, and since the gifts were designed to reveal and confirm the faith as it was being revealed by the inspired men (Jude 3; Heb. 2:3-4), the gifts have fulfilled their functions and have ceased. The Incarnation of Christ, the cross, the resurrection, and the making of the offering in heaven were once for all. These are not repeated in each generation. The work of the apostles and prophets was the continuation of Christ's work in that it dealt with the revelation and confirmation of the will of Christ. They were guided into all the truth (John 16:13-14), and unless this was done during their lifetime Jesus' promise failed. The complete truth was delivered in the first century, and thereby the faith was once for all delivered to the saints. It is not delivered anew each century. That faith is recorded in the Bible and we should study it, believe in it, live by it and contend for it. The Christ and His will, which was revealed in the first century, are the complete revelation of God to man and we find our completeness in Him. (Col. 2:3-4, 9-10)

Chapter VI

What Shall We Do?

As we are confronted with the threat of Pentecostalism, what are some of the things which we should do? *First*, we must stress the fact that there is sufficient reason to believe in Christ today without having to have miracles today. Every person — even an atheist — has some sort of faith on which he is staking his life. There are some difficulties which the Christian faces, but they are not such that they should undermine faith in God, Christ, and the Bible. During the personal ministry of Christ, Peter realized there were some difficulties, but he also realized that Jesus was the Christ and if they turned from Him there was no one else to whom they could go. (John 6:60-69) The credentials of Christ are sufficient although they do not force one to believe. (1) His miracles which were acknowledged even by His enemies. (Matt. 12:22-24; Acts 2:22) The record of these miracles is enshrined in documents which stand the tests which can legitimately be applied to documents. (2) The fulfillment of prophecies which were uttered centuries before His coming. An entire series of such prophecies is found in Isaiah 53. (3) The testimony of His marvelous personality and life; even many infidels find no fault in Him. (4) The testimony of His moral and spiritual teaching which have not been surpassed. (5) The evidence for the resurrection. This testimony was borne by reliable witnesses and is recorded in trustworthy documents. (6) The impact of His life and teaching on the world, i.e., by His fruits you can know Him. (7) By the fact that in a real sense His way of life works and no other way really works. This is an aspect of the test of results, of fruits. (8) There is a testimony which comes in the crucible of experience as we live the Christian life. This is related to point seven. There is the deep of His teaching which calls to the deep of our own being. He calls forth in us possibilities of which we were really unaware, or only vaguely realized. There is a proof of the pudding which is found in the eating thereof. Through this we become more and more assured that He who made us also gave us the Book and the Christ. (9) There is also the fact that if we turn from Christ, we turn to far greater difficulties than some find in connection with Christ; and we do not find in others any such wide range of convincing credentials. (10) Human history and personal experience continue to verify Jesus' claim to be the light of the world. (John 8:12) One can test the claims of Christ by accepting and walking by each truth which he sees, and continuing to study and learn additional truths. In this way, we are convinced, men can be led step by step to Christ. By walking in the light one is led on to additional light.

It is the author's conviction that study and experience will increasingly confirm for one the truth of Peter's statement in John 6:67-69.

STUDY THE SCRIPTURES

We should study the Scriptures. We need to be honest in our study of the Scriptures and if we are wrong in this matter we should accept the gift of tongues. However, if we accept it as being from God we should accept it publicly. The Holy Spirit would not leave us so confused that we did not understand the primary purpose of tongues, nor would the Spirit lead us into a position which, in effect, deceived brethren. The very confusion of these brethren, along this line, is proof they do not have the miraculous gift or gifts of the Spirit.

By studying the Scriptures we shall not only be built up in the faith but also protected against error.

HAVING AND BEING A PROBLEM

We should distinguish between those who are confused, but are not advocating Pentecostalism. We should study with them as long as is necessary. However, those who advocate it must be talked with, and if we cannot change them they should be withdrawn from before they cause a greater division in the church than they have already caused.

TEACHING

Although one should not camp on just one subject, Pentecostalism needs to be dealt with from the pulpit, in class studies, in

WHAT SHALL WE DO?

private studies, and in making available written material on the subject.

LIVE BY THE TRUTH

We must not only contend for the truth but also live by the truth. We should demonstrate love and concern for others. We should realize that the Bible is a sword but it is also the word which must be used to comfort, to strengthen, to encourage, to uplift people, and to instruct them in the new life in Christ. (Titus 2:11-14; 1 Thess. 5:14-15)

PRAYER

While making clear that we do not believe that we have miraculous power (Acts 1:8; 2:22), we should also make it clear that we believe that God does hear and answer prayer. He may say, Yes; He may say, No, or He may say, Wait awhile. But we should make it clear that we do not believe that God has left us here as orphans.

DO GOOD

It is not always exciting or dramatic, but Christians should realize that they are to go about doing good. One young man, who had become involved in the Pentecostalism in the church, wrote my wife and told how that even during the time he was being so aggressive for the gifts he had not found peace. One of the things, however, which had stuck in his mind were the simple acts of hospitality which we had extended to him when he spent the night in our home while on a Chorus trip from a college in a different state. Emotions can burn out, excitement can wear off, but walking by His word and doing good day by day is the best demonstration and proof of the power of Christ in our lives.

We are not suggesting that Pentecostals do not teach that one is to do good. We are saying that the gifts were a means to the end of revealing the truth, but that the moral fruit of the Spirit in our lives is to be borne throughout the gospel dispensation. (Gal. 5:16, 22-23)

JOY

Let us try to grow in the joys of the new life in Christ. While realizing our duties and responsibilities let us also rejoice because of our privileges and promises. The written word can make our joy full. (1 John 1:1-4) Enrich the emotional life but keep it under the control of the word of God and the mind.

EXPRESS CONCERN AND APPRECIATION

Do not be afraid to show concern for others, or to express appreciation. By our lives let us try to demonstrate that love worketh no ill (Rom. 13:8-10), but that it works good toward others. (Matt. 7:12; 1 Cor. 13)

SPIRITUALITY IS NOT AN EMOTION

While it is true that Christianity enriches, disciplines, and refines our emotional life, and while chills may sometimes run up and down our spines as we sing the songs of Zion, it is not true that spirituality is an emotion. We have not become spiritual because we turn down the lights, hold hands, and get an emotional reaction. We are spiritual if we live by the word of Christ which includes that which at times may be emotionally distasteful duties.

Peter said that Christians "as living stones, are built up a spiritual house, to be a holy priesthood to offer up spiritual sacrifices, acceptable to God through Jesus Christ." "But ye are an elect race, a royal priesthood, a holy nation, a people for God's own possession, that ye may show forth the excellencies of him who called you out of darkness into his marvellous light: who in time past were no people, but now are the people of God: who had not obtained mercy, but now have obtained mercy." (1 Pet. 2:5, 9, 10)

What are these spiritual sacrifices? They involve material things, although they must be offered from the heart. As the following passages show, our spirituality is measured not by our emotional mood at a given time, but by whether we are a royal priesthood offering up the sacrifices sincerely and therefore from the heart. The church, of course, is the spiritual house or temple. (Eph. 2:19-22)

Our bodies are offered to God as a living sacrifice, and this means that our body members must be used as instruments of righteousness. (Rom. 12:1-2; 6:12-13) The spiritual person may sometimes be on the heights of emotional delight, but his spirituality is measured by whether or not he goes about doing good and refrains from using his body members as instruments of unrighteousness. The doing of good is a sacrifice. "But to do good and to communicate forget not: for with such sacrifices God is well pleased." (Heb. 13:16)

To communicate, I think, includes extending material aid when necessary. Therefore, Paul spoke of the contributions from

Philippi as "an odor of a sweet smell, a sacrifice acceptable, well-pleasing to God." (Phil. 4:18) While some view money as material and not related to spirituality, Paul shows that how we use our money is an index to our spirituality. Therefore, we are not amazed when he passes from a discussion of the resurrection of the dead in 1 Corinthians 15, to remarks concerning the collection for the saints. (1 Cor. 16:1) Among the numerous motivating appeals which he made to Corinth to stimulate them to give, he used what Christ gave up for us (which included, although he did not mention it, his death on the cross). (2 Cor. 8:9)

Another sacrifice which we offer through Christ is "a sacrifice of praise to God continually, that is, the fruit of lips which make confession to his name." (Heb. 13:15)

The spiritual person is described in the beatitudes. He may be deeply moved, for he mourns concerning his sins, but unless this leads to repentance and the acceptance of God's mercy the mourner will not be comforted. To put it another way, the spiritual person is the one who loves God with all of his being, and his neighbor as himself. Negatively speaking, love refrains from evil. (Rom. 13:8-10) Positively speaking, love does the good unto the other that one wants done unto himself. (Matt. 7:12)

We are not minimizing the enrichment and the control of the emotions. It feels good to feel good! Feeling can help motivate us. A good feeling, however, does not mean that one is spiritual. If the good feeling flows from doing good, it is connected with our spiritual sacrifice, but within itself it is not a proof of our spirituality.

Do you seek spirituality? Then from the heart offer unto God, as a spiritual priest, the sacrifices which God has ordained for the gospel age. When these are accompanied by emotional reactions you may enjoy these reactions, but do not base spirituality on the ebb and flow of emotionalism. In fact, our emotions are the most unstable part about us, and the least to be depended on as a guide to righteousness and worship in spirit and in truth.

Chapter VII

A Review of "They Speak With Other Tongues"

John L. Sherrill recorded his conversion to the tongues movement in *They Speak With Other Tongues*. We are reviewing this book for two reasons. *First,* it contains many of the arguments used by the people involved in the tongues movement in the church. *Second,* in a letter on March 26, 1970 Pat Boone told me that this book was "one of the milestones in my odyssey. . . ." Pat is the best known person among us who espouses these views, and hundreds of thousands of copies of his book have been published. Over a year ago we sent Sherrill copies of these comments.

At least in part Sherrill's book is based on the existential approach which runs down the mind and logic and views the "leap of faith" as the way to faith in Christ. In speaking of a certain experience he wrote: "Once before I had passed from intellectual inquiry, to the presence of the thing itself, and then on to something almost like physical contact. But that is the story of the book. . . ." (p. 7)

LAY ASIDE LOGIC

In the midst of a crisis in his health, Sherrill heard a young seminarian speak at St. Thomas Episcopal Church on Fifth Avenue. "I didn't know it then, but this brief address was to hold the key to the most astonishing experience of my life.

"At the time it seemed wretchedly irrelevant to my problem. The young man gave a short talk on Nicodemus. Many of us try, he said, to approach Christ as Nicodemus did: through logic. 'Rabbi, we know that you are a teacher sent by God,' Nicodemus said, and then he gave his reason — a logical one: . . . no one could perform these signs of yours unless God were with him.'

" 'But, you see, said the seminarian, 'as long as Nicodemus was trying to come to an understanding of Christ through his logic, he could never succeed. It isn't logic, but an experience, that lets us know who Christ is. Christ, Himself, told Nicodemus this: 'In very truth I tell you, unless a man has been born over again he cannot see the kingdom of God.' " (Sherrill, 10)

First, although one would need to test a teacher by his teaching also, as far as he went Nicodemus' logic was excellent. Nicodemus was logical and right in his conclusion that Jesus' signs showed that God was with Jesus. *The next logical step* was that since Jesus is the teacher sent from God, men should accept His teaching concerning God, Himself, the Kingdom, the Spirit, man, and on any other subject on which Jesus speaks.

Second, Nicodemus' logic was not only good but it was approved of God, since the very reason that God gave Jesus these signs was to confirm Jesus as the teacher sent from God; and, among other things, Jesus taught that He is God's son. John makes this clear when he affirms that even the record of the signs was *designed by God* to produce faith that Jesus is the Christ. (John 20:30-31) Through the inspiration of the Holy Spirit Peter declared: "Ye men of Israel, hear these words: Jesus of Nazareth, a man *approved of God* unto you by mighty (powers) works and wonders and signs *which God did by him in the midst of you,* even as ye yourselves know." (Acts 2:22) Concerning the word "approved", W. E. Vine wrote: literally "to point out, to exhibit . . . is used once in the sense of proving by demonstration, and so bringing about an approval." Furthermore, the Spirit through Peter appealed to the miracles on Pentecost — the sound, the tongues like as of fire, and the speaking in foreign languages — as one of the grounds on which men were justified in believing in Christ. (Acts 2:33) Two other lines of evidence were presented on Pentecost; the fulfillment of prophecy, and the witness of the apostles to the resurrected Christ. On the basis of these lines of evidence, what *logical* conclusion was drawn? "Let all the house of Israel *therefore know assuredly,* that God hath made him both Lord and Christ, this Jesus whom ye crucified." (Acts 2:36) In all of this the apostles were appealing to the minds of men. This is clear from the fact that more than once Peter called for their attention to what was being said. (Acts 2:14, 22, 29) Having presented the evidence, Peter called on the audience to accept the logical conclusion that Jesus is the Christ. Did any of them accept this logical conclusion? "Now when they heard, they were pricked in their heart, and said unto Peter and the rest of the apostles, Brethren, what shall we do?" (Acts 2:36) Words told them what to do, words exhorted them to do it, and they that gladly received the word did it. (Acts 2:38-41) The reader is reminded that the "heart" is often used in the Bible to refer to the thinking and willing aspects of man's nature.

If the apostle Peter had been Sherrill, who endorsed the idea contained in the quotation from his book, he would have replied to the questioners in Acts 2:37 by saying: "When such logical conclusions are drawn and accepted, one is trying to approach Christ through logic. This can never succeed. What you must do is to have an experience." Even if this were the case, the audience would have had to use their mind and logic to realize that the logical approach was wrong, to understand that they must have an experience, to understand the type of experience they were to have, to understand how to seek for the experience, and to know when they had received the experience. Without logic and the mind we could not understand the nature of our experiences.

Nicodemus, in the logical approach which he made, was simply responding with a good and honest heart to *God's own appeal* to Nicodemus' mind and logic. If Sherrill had the miraculous guidance of the Spirit, he would have known that there was nothing wrong with Nicodemus' approach. He would have known that through signs God confirmed the word. (Mk. 16:19, 20) Or his friends, who claim to have the Spirit in a miraculous way, should have pointed out this very significant and serious error.

Third, Jesus did not tell Nicodemus that Nicodemus could not know who Jesus was through logic and, therefore, he must learn it through an experience. Christ said that Nicodemus could not enter into, he could not see, participate in, or enjoy the kingdom, unless he was born again. In fact, unless one first believes that Jesus is the Christ, he cannot enter into the kingdom. How could one be translated into the kingdom of God's Son if he did not first believe that Jesus is God's Son? (Col. 1:13) The gospel must be preached. The hearing of the gospel leads to faith. Those who believe are to be baptized into Christ. (Mk. 16:15-16; Rom. 10:17; Matt. 28:19) Faith is basic in the new birth, but baptism is also a part of the new birth. (John 3:5; Gal. 3:26-27) Faith in Christ comes before baptism into Christ.

Fourth, it is true that Nicodemus, even though he realized Jesus was a teacher sent from God, did not understand everything about Jesus. He was puzzled by the teaching concerning the new birth, and did not believe — likely because he did not understand — certain things. (John 3:9-12) However, in this he was not unlike the apostles who were confused, ignorant, and unbelieving concerning some things during the personal ministry. This was true, even though they believed Jesus is the Christ. (Matt. 16:16-17, 21-23; Lk. 9:45; Lk. 24:25-26) In all that He said to Nicodemus, however, Jesus did not condemn the logic whereby Nicodemus concluded that Jesus was sent of God.

Fifth, when the evidence, which comes through hearing the word of God, leads to faith (Rom. 10:17), one should submit to God's will and undergo the *experience* of the birth. In fact, faith is a vital part of this experience. In becoming servants of righteousness we obey from the heart. (John 3:2-5; Rom. 6:2-5, 17-18) By living the new life we experience the meaning of the new life.

There are reasons to eat the pudding and there is also proof of the pudding in the eating thereof.

1 CORINTHIANS 14

Although it is often overlooked, the very thrust of the regulations concerning the miraculous gifts in Corinth was that unless the gifts were used so as to reach and instruct the mind they were not being used properly. Tongues were not to be used, when no one present understood, because understanding is essential to edification. (14:2-6) After using the illustration of the uncertain sounds, Paul said: "So also ye, unless ye utter by the tongues speech easy to be *understood,* how shall it be *known* what is spoken? for ye will be speaking into the air." (14:9) To speak in such a way as to block communication with the understanding of others was to treat them as a barbarian. (14:11) Unless the listener understand what you say, he cannot agree with it even if you are speaking truth in a tongue; for "he knoweth not what thou sayest." (14:16) Therefore Paul had "rather speak five words with my understanding, that I might instruct others also, than ten thousands words in a tongue." (14:19) Prophecy was greater than the gift of tongues because "he that prophesieth speaketh unto man edification, and exhortation, and consolation." (14:3, 5) Tongues when translated, either by the speaker or by someone else, reached the understanding and, in such cases, edified the church. (14:5, 26-28)

Reason and logic are involved in hearing, understanding, believing, and obeying the gospel. Although faith goes beyond reason and logic, any approach to the Bible which lays aside logic is an unscriptural approach. Furthermore, even this approach is presented to the mind and must be understood and acted on by the mind.

THE LEAP OF FAITH

In response to an urgent request from a friend who had heard of his imminent operation, John L. Sherrill and his wife went to the home of the friend. This friend asked if he believed Jesus was God. His father had been a professor at Union Theological Seminary, and Sherrill viewed himself as a nominal Christian. He had never come to grips with this question, and when asked this question, he tried to come to grips with it, but "there were mountains of logic which halted me. I started to map them for Catherine, but she stopped me.

" 'You're trying to approach Christianity through your mind, John,' she said. 'It simply can't be done that way.'

"There it was again. Catherine went on. 'It's one of the peculiarities of Christianity that you cannot come to it through intellect. You have to be willing to experience it first, to do something you don't understand — and then oddly enough, understanding often follows. And it's just that which I'm hoping for you today . . . that without understanding, without even knowing why, you say "Yes" to Christ.'

"There was silence in the room. I had an eternity of reservations. And at the same time I had a sudden desire to do precisely what she was suggesting."

On his way home, as they drove down the road, he turned to his wife and said: "'What do they call it: "a leap of faith"? All right, I'm going to make the leap: I believe that Christ was God.'

"It was a cold-blooded laying down of my sense of what was logcial, quite without emotional conviction. And with it went something that was essentially 'me.' All the bundle of self-consciousness that we call our ego seemed somehow involved in this decision. It was amazing how much it hurt, how desperately this thing fought for life, so that there was a real kind of death involved. But when it was dead and quiet finally, and I blurted out my simple statement of belief, there was room in me for something new and altogether mysterious." (John L. Sherrill, *They Speak With Other Tongues*, p. 11)

It is obvious that Mr. Sherrill had an experience. We shall not deny that the experience was real, but real experiences as well as imaginary ones must be evaluated by the word of God. We are to be judged by Christ and His word, and not just by our experiences. (John 12:48; Acts 17:31)

MIND CANNOT BE BY-PASSED

In one's approach to Christianity it is impossible to by-pass the mind. The mind would have to be used to decide that one cannot approach Christianity through one's mind. One would have to study, and learn something about Christianity to know that "one of the peculiarities of Christianity" is "that you cannot come to it through intellect." One would have to use his mind to realize that one must do something that he did not understand, that he would then experience Christianity, and then understanding often follows. One would have to know that, without even knowing why, he should say "Yes" to Christ. Not only would one have to understand this much, but he would have to believe that it was at least worth the effort to try this way.

CHRISTIANITY APPEALS TO THE MIND

Christianity involves faith, but reasons for faith are also involved. The evidence which we have justifies us in believing that Jesus is the Christ. Trusting in Christ we walk by faith and not by sight, but our minds were involved in accepting Christ in the first place, and in understanding His will and living the new life in Christ by faith in the second place.

Christ appeals to the mind of the unbeliever in leading him to faith, and to the mind of the believer in guiding him in the new life. *First,* consider the appeal to the mind of the unbeliever. The man who rejects God is a fool. (Psa. 14:1) He is a fool not because he uses his mind, but because he refuses to use his mind to draw the logical conclusion from the existence of the universe; including the existence of man himself. God has manifested Himself. "For the invisible things of him since the creation of the world are clearly seen, being perceived through the things that are made, even his everlasting power and divinity; that they may be without excuse: because that, knowing God, they glorified him not as God, neither gave thanks; but became *vain in their reasonings,* and their *senseless* heart was darkened. Professing themselves to be wise, they became fools. . . ." (Rom. 1:20-23) When the mind of man is condemned it is because it has been misused, and man has turned to vain reasonings which leave him with a darkened, senseless heart. The wisdom of the world, which is condemned, is that determination of man to understand all through the human mind without divine revelation.

However, the fact that man can misuse the mind does not mean that God does not appeal to man to use his mind honestly in dealing with the facts and the evidences which confront man. To bring forth fruit, the seed of truth must be sown in good and honest hearts. Men must not misuse their faculties, but use their eyes to see, their ears to hear, and their hearts to understand. (Matt. 13:16, 23; Lk. 8:15) If we fail to do this, we shall fail to turn to the Great Physician and be healed. (Matt. 13:15) Therefore, when the apostles went forth sowing the seed, as they were guided and inspired by the Spirit, they taught people, they reasoned with them, they presented evidence, and they persuaded them. (Acts 2:36-41; 17:11-12; 18:4, 5, 11) Faith comes by hearing the word of God, and this word of God presented Christ and His credentials, and thereby gave men reasons to believe. We indeed make a leap of faith, but we do not leap from unbelief to faith without having any reasons to come to faith in Christ. Having believed in Christ, we do leap by faith and trusting Him we live by faith. Faith goes beyond sight but there are sufficient reasons to justify faith doing this.

Second, after we have accepted Christ the mind is still appealed to by the Spirit through the Scriptures. In fact, we are to love God with all our *mind* as well as with the rest of our being. (Matt. 22:37) The mind is appealed to in teaching Christians to observe what Jesus commanded. (Matt. 28:20) The epistles appeal to the mind and understanding of the readers. To the Thessalonians, Paul wrote: "I adjure you by the Lord that this epistle be read unto all the brethren." (5:27) To the Colossians he said: "And when this epistle hath been read among you, cause that it be read also in the church of the Laodiceans; and that ye also read the epistle from Laodicea." (Col. 4:16) Although there are some things that are difficult (2 Pet. 3:17-18), Paul said to the Ephesians: "when ye read, ye can perceive my understanding in the mystery of Christ." (Eph. 3:4) He also stressed: "Wherefore be ye not foolish, but understand what the will of the Lord is." (5:17) When we read the written word we are listening to the voice of God, the voice of the Spirit, and the voice of the apostles and prophets. (Matt. 22:31; Lk. 16:29-31; Acts 13:27; Heb. 10:15; Rev. 2:1, 7)

SHERRILL'S CONFESSION OF FAITH

The author does not know all that is involved in Sherrill's concept of Christ as God. Christ is divine. He is God's Son, although He is not God the Father. To truly confess Jesus Christ one must believe it in his heart before he confesses it with his lips. He does not, according to the Bible, confess it with his lips and then believe it in his heart. Although in Rom. 10:9 Paul mentioned confession before he mentioned faith in the heart, he makes it clear that faith in the heart came before confession with the lips. How could unbelieving lips confess faith in Christ? Paul wrote: "The word is nigh thee, *in thy mouth, and in thy heart:* that is, the *word of faith, which we preach:* because if thou shalt confess with thy mouth Jesus as Lord, and shalt believe in thy heart that God raised him from the dead, thou shalt be saved: for with the heart man believeth unto righteousness; and with the mouth confession is made unto salvation." One must call on the Lord in order to be saved. "How then shall they call on him *in whom they have not believed?* and how shall they believe in him whom they have not heard? and how shall they hear without a preacher?" "So belief cometh of hearing, and hearing by the word of Christ." (Rom. 10:8-10, 13, 14, 17)

Sherrill had enough faith to make a leap of faith and to say: "I believe that Christ was God." He laid aside his pride to say it, and felt a sense of release when he did so. Faith when expressed can increase faith. This is true, even when one has faith in the wrong thing or the wrong person. The Mormons, for example, strengthen their faith in the prophetship of Joseph Smith, Jr. by affirming that Joseph Smith, Jr. was a prophet of God, and that the Book of Mormon is of divine origin, and this is their testimony which they give unto us.

The author does not doubt the sincerity of Sherrill's faith, but he is confident that the Bible teaches that Christianity does approach us through the mind, and, therefore, we approach Christianity through the mind. Although the mind, without the divine revelation and the evidence which confirms it, could never of itself know the mind of God, yet God has revealed His mind through the Word taught by men inspired by the Spirit. (1 Cor. 2:10-13) Whatever degree of faith we have at any time, we should exercise it, and should continue to study the Bible. When we learn more, and as our faith grows, we should continue to act by faith on what we learn. Faith, when expressed in word and in deeds, is encouraged to grow. Faith unexpressed tends to die. Leaping by faith, but there are reasons to leap, and walking by faith are followed by additional confirmation as the proof of the pudding is more and more found in the eating of the pudding. However, there are good reasons for us to start eating in the first place.

Later on Mr. Sherrill thought that he received the baptism of the Spirit, and the gift of tongues, but he remained within the Episcopal Church. The Spirit in the first century did not leave men in, or lead men to, some denominational group, but led them into Christ's body, which is His church. The Spirit is against denominationalism. (John 17:20-21; Eph. 1:20-23; 4:1-6; 1 Cor. 1:10-13) Therefore, we confidently affirm there is something seriously wrong with a man's claim of an experience of the baptism, and miraculous guidance, of the Spirit when he is left in denominationalism and, thereby, continues to help prevent the Lord's prayer for unity. (John 17:20-21) This is not said to question anyone's sincerity, but their understanding of the will of God; and their interpretation of certain of their experiences.

As those of old, we must always go to the law and to the testimony (Isa. 8:20)

DID HE SEE THE LORD?

The second night after a very critical and painful operation, John L. Sherrill awoke in the middle of the night and became aware of an unusual light which was "more of an illumination than a light with a defined source. But there was something remarkable about this light: it had, somehow, a center of awareness." Without moving from where it was the light was suddenly closer to him, and although his pain did not go away he felt as if he were bursting with health. He thought it was Christ, and he asked that the boy in the room, who was groaning, be helped. Without leaving him, the light seemed beside the boy's bed and the boy became silent. At Sherrill's request the light moved to the bed of an old man who was coughing, and the coughing stopped. Then the light left. He stayed awake until dawn, but felt rested. When he finally told his wife about it, they both thought it could not be a dream.

When he related it to two very close friends, one of them asked if he saw the light again. He had not. " 'I don't think you should expect to, either,' she said. 'This kind of face to face meeting with Christ usually happens just once. It happened to me in a way very like yours. With Len it was entirely different. But it's that certain recognition of Christ that's the amazing thing, however it happens.'

"And then Catherine said an interesting thing. As it turned out, it was a kind of prophecy. 'I'm glad you told us. It will help fix it in your own mind, for the time when it no longer seems real.' She smiled a little wistfully. 'I wish there were some way to feel always as you do now. As far as I know, there isn't. Once we lose the freshness of that first meeting, we just have to walk by faith.' " (*They Speak With Other Tongues,* Old Tappan, New Jersey: Fleming H. Revell Co., 1964, pp. 13-15)

Although we should be willing to listen to Mr. Sherrill's experience, as well as those of others, we must prove all things and hold fast that which is good, and which does not go contrary to the Scriptures. (Acts 17:11-12; 1 Thess. 5:21; 2 Thess. 2:15) We must continue in the apostles' doctrine. (John 12:48; Matt. 28:20; Acts 2:42; 1 Cor. 14:37)

QUESTION NEITHER SINCERITY NOR THE FACT OF AN EXPERIENCE

In evaluating Mr. Sherrill's experience we do not question his sincerity. Furthermore, we do not question the fact that he had an experience, nor that the experience had a tremendous impact on him. One may question an *interpretation of an experience* while granting that the person has sincerely experienced something. The author lost his father and his mother in a train-car accident in 1927. B. C. Goodpasture and Brother James McBroom participated in the funeral services. As a boy of eleven the author was taken into the home of his grandparents. With a vividness which is not undimmed by the passing of well over forty years, the author recalls an experience. He awoke early one morning. Sometimes one may then pass from an awakened condition to that of sleep and dream, and also pass back rapidly. The author thought he was awake. He saw his mother come in the door of the room, walk to his bedside, put her hand on his head, and then depart without saying a word. He does not recall awakening after this experience. It seemed to be a real event taking place while he was awake. This type of experience never happened again. He has dreamed of his parents but never under such conditions. However, the author is convinced that it was a dream.

During World War II the author heard H. G. Wells speak in San Francisco, California. After the lecture he met Mr. Wells. A few other people met him also. After Wells left, the author chatted with one of these individuals. He was a retired British naval officer, and a member of the Church of the New Jerusalem. (Swedenborg). He told the author that the Lord Jesus was visiting him regularly and sitting for His portrait. The author does not know what the explanation of these experiences was, for the man seemed sincere. However, in many situations even if one does not know the explanation he can be confident that certain explanations are false. One may not know who a certain woman is, but he may be certain that she is not his wife. We must test all by the Bible, and not let anyone's experience become the authority for us; nor should they let their experiences be the authority for them. The faith has once for all been delivered unto the saints (Jude 3), and we must measure all by it. Regardless of how sincere the man in San Francisco was, we know that if the Lord appeared to someone today He would appear for some purpose other than having His portrait painted.

When we go to the Bible we find that the Lord did appear to Saul. Let us contrast the experiences of Saul with those of Mr. Sherrill.

SAUL SAW THE LORD JESUS CHRIST

First, Saul stated that the last post-resurrection appearance of Jesus was to him. After His resurrection "he *appeared* to Cephas; then to the twelve; then he *appeared* to about five hundred brethren at once, of whom the greater part remain until now, but some are fallen asleep; then he *appeared* to James; then to all the apostles; and *last of all,* as to the child untimely born, he *appeared to me also."* (1 Cor. 15:5-8) Christ promised to appear to Saul in some additional matters (Acts 26:16), but there is no scriptural evidence that anyone else after Paul had such a face to face encounter with Christ. We are not saying that none of the other apostles had no visions or revelations, for John had a vision after our Lord appeared to Saul. (Rev. 2:13-18) However, there are no indications of any appearances of Jesus to any additional people, who had not already seen Him, after His appearance to Saul. Paul said: "and *last of all* . . . He appeared to me also." Sherrill saw some sort of light. He did not see Christ Himself.

Second, there were no miracles which confirmed the appearance which Mr. Sherrill thought he experienced, but miracles did confirm Christ's appearance to Saul. (a) In broad day light, around noon, while Saul was traveling "suddenly, there shone from heaven a great light around me." (Acts 22:6) It was "above the brightness of the sun." (Acts 26:12) (b) Those who were with Saul saw the light. The light, Saul said, was "shining round about me and them that journeyed with me." (26:13) "And they that were with me beheld indeed the light, but they heard not the voice of Him that spake to me." (Acts 22:9) (c) A voice *spoke* to Saul, and *conversed* with Saul. (Acts 9:4, 7; 22:7, 10; 26:14-18) (d) Those who were with Saul did not hear the voice in the sense of understanding what was said (22:9), but they did hear in the sense of hearing the sound. "And the men that journeyed with him stood speechless, hearing the voice, but beholding no man." (9:7) (e) Saul was blinded (22:11; 9:8), and later was instantaneously healed. (9:12, 18; 22:13) (f) Saul later had miraculous confirmation for Christ enabled him to work a wide variety of miracles. (g) He had additional miraculous confirmation in that Christ gave him the power to confer miraculous gifts on others. (Acts 19:1-7; Rom. 1:11) The differences between the appearance to Saul, and the experience of Sherrill, are clear. After the appearance Sherrill was still in a hospital bed, his two roommates were still confined to the hospital, and although Sherrill left the hospital "a full week earlier than Dr. Catlin had predicted," it took him some time to mend. Later he does think he received tongues.

Athough no one in the hospital was healed that night, although no one received perfect soundness (Acts 3:16; 4:10), Sherrill thought that "The stories of healing (in the Bible, J.D.B.) were like reliving that night in the hospital." (*They Speak With Other Tongues,* p. 16)

Third, Saul received a message from the Lord, when the Lord appeared to him. He was told to go into the city and there it would be told him what he must do. (Acts 9:6) Furthermore, he was told that Christ would make further appearances to him and give him additional instruction. (Acts 26:16-17) Saul learned the gospel not from man but by revelation of Jesus Christ; and this is the way he learned all of the New Testament truth which he taught. "For I make known to you, brethren, as touching the gospel which was preached by me, that it is not after man. For neither did I receive it from man, nor was I taught it, but (it came to me) through revelation of Jesus Christ." (Gal. 1:11-12) To the Corinthians he wrote: "For I delivered unto you first of all that which also I received: that Christ. . . ." (15:3) How did Paul learn about the Lord's supper? "For I received of the Lord that which also I delivered unto you, that the Lord Jesus in the night in which he was betrayed took bread. . . ." (1 Cor. 11:23) Saul spoke by inspiration. God revealed and confirmed truth through Saul. (Heb. 2:3-4) Therefore, he spoke with authority and men were bound by what he taught. (1 Cor. 14:37; 2 Thess. 2:15; 3:4, 6, 12, 14)

Sherrill did not learn the gospel by direct revelation. There is no real proof that he speaks inspired messages which men are bound to obey.

Fourth, Saul wrote inspired scripture. The word which Paul spoke was inspired, and so was the word which he wrote. ". . . the things which I write unto you, that they are the commandment of the Lord." (1 Cor. 14:37) "So, then, brethren, stand fast, and hold the traditions which ye were taught, whether by word, or by epistle of ours." (2 Thess. 2:15) Sherrill does not even claim, so far as we know, to write inspired scripture. Why wasn't *They Speak With Other Tongues* inspired?

Fifth, Saul's experience was corroborated by the experience of Ananias. Saul was sent into the city to wait for instructions as to what he must do. (Acts 9:6-9) There is no indication that Ananias, who did not become an apostle of Christ, saw the Lord in the sense that Saul did; but he did have a vision. ". . . the Lord said unto him in a vision. . . ." He was told where to find Saul; on the street called Straight and in the house of Judas. He was also told what Saul was doing — praying. Ananias was sent to Saul. (Acts 9:10-11) Saul was informed that Ananias was coming. Saul was also told why Ananias would lay hands on him. "And he hath seen a man named Ananias coming in, and laying his hands on him, *that* he might receive his sight." (Acts 9:12) This was additional corroboration to Saul. His experience was further confirmed when Ananias laid hands on him, and he did receive his sight *immediately.* (Acts 9:12, 17)

There was no such corroboration of Sherrill's experience.

Sixth, Saul was placed in contact with someone who told him what to do to be saved. "But rise, and enter into the city, and it shall be told thee what thou must do." (Acts 9:6) He was told a number of things (Acts 22:10), but one of the things which he was told very quickly was to be baptized. "And now why tarriest thou? arise, and be baptized, and wash away thy sins, calling on His name." (Acts 22:16) This baptism was unto the remission of sins and into the body of Christ. (Acts 2:38; John 3:5) Saul himself taught that it was into Christ's death, a burial with Christ, and a resurrection to the new life in Christ. (Rom. 6:2-5; Gal. 3:26-27) There was no long period of time between the time Ananias came to him and the time he was baptized. After he received his sight, "he arose and was baptized." (9:18) Athough it had been three days between the time of the appearance of the Lord, and Saul's baptism, he had not eaten nor drunk (9:9, 19), and there was no such elapse of time between the time he learned what he was to do with reference to baptism, and his baptism.

Mr. Sherrill was not placed in contact with someone who baptized him. As far as we know, he still has not learned the New Testament teaching on baptism.

Seventh, Saul was not left in Judaism but became a member of the New Testament church in being baptized into Christ. Sherrill was left in the Episcopal Church even after he later received what he thought was the gift of tongues.

Eighth, Sherrill's teaching concerning baptism, denominationalism, and some other matters, we are confident, can be shown to be out of harmony with the teaching of those in the New Testament to whom the Lord did appear. If men today have the same type of experience, why do they not teach the same doctrine?

Ninth, the Lord's appearance to Saul was involved in Saul's becoming an apostle. (Gal. 1:1-2; Acts 22:15) "But arise, and stand upon thy feet: for *to this end* have I appeared unto thee, to appoint thee a minister and a witness both of the things wherein thou hast seen me, and of the things wherein I will appear unto thee; delivering thee from the people, and from the Gentiles, unto whom I send thee. . . ." (Acts 26:16-17) Later Paul said: "for he that wrought for Peter unto the apostleship of the circumcision wrought for me also unto the Gentiles." (Gal. 2:8)

Sherrill did not become an apostle of Christ with the qualifications, the power, the authority, and the mission which belonged to Christ's apostles.

It may be objected that the Lord's appearance to someone today does not have to match in every detail Christ's appearances in the first century. One does not have to argue for every detail in order to argue that there should be enough parallels to prove that what has happened to someone today was an actual appearance of Jesus Christ.

If someone else claims that they experience an appearance of an angel of the Lord, rather than of Jesus Christ, one could make a close study and compare it, in some of the categories mentioned in connection with Saul's case. He could show how the experience of Peter was corroborated by that of Cornelius, the miracles which were involved, the additional truth which was revealed, and the fact that such an experience as that of Cornelius' household was not repeated.

The author does not believe that Mr. Sherrill's experience was a supernatural one. He does not have to know which particular natural explanation explains the experience in order to know that it does not parallel what the Bible teaches about Christ's post-resurrection appearances. All things must be measured not by an individual's sincerity or experience, but by the Bible.

THE TUMBLING WALLS

In a chapter on "The Walls Came Tumbling Down," John L. Sherrill in *They Speak With Other Tongues* sets forth some of his insights and observations based on experiences in connection with his research into, and conversion to, the tongues movement.

A NEW TYPE OF PENTECOSTAL

While Sherrill was feeling as if the Pentecostals had no answer, he established contact with a new type of Pentecostal; one who became involved in the movement with his family as a child in 1908. While a young adult he became a Pentecostal minister "who knew who the enemies were: sin, the devil, and liberal churchmen." (p. 53) For many years, he and others "contributed building blocks to the wall of misunderstanding separating the Pentecostals from the old-line churches." Everything was black and white to him, and people were either "villains or heroes." He refused to listen to anyone else. During times of meditation during his recovery, which took weeks, from an automobile accident he concluded this approach was wrong, and he should be willing to listen to others. He became one "who talked lovingly and not accusingly to people of other traditions." (pp. 52, 54-55) He felt he was led to "let the walls down," and "hold out the hand of friendship to any who will take it." He was convinced he was led by God to approach the World Council of Churches, the "very headquarters of the most liberal, the most intellectual, the most ecumenically minded of modernists." (p. 56)

The degree of his change, not merely in attitude and approach, but also in his view of modernism and of the traditional churches is indicated by his repy to the question of an Episcopal priest. He was asked: "Are you telling us that you Pentecostals have the truth, and we other churches do not?" His reply was that: "We both have the truth." He illustrated that there is a difference in a steak frozen solid, and one on the fire with its delicious aroma. " 'Gentlemen,' said David, 'that is the difference between our ways of handling the same truth. You have yours on ice; we have ours on fire.' " (pp. 58, 59)

There are lessons, as well as warnings, in the experiences of David du Plessis, the new Pentecostal of whom Sherrill wrote.

TRUTH IN LOVE

First, it is possible to possess truth and yet not rightly approach others who do not have certain truths which you accept. Not only are we to live truth in love, but also *speak* it to others in the same spirit of love. (Eph. 4:15) To love is to will good toward. Speaking the truth in love means speaking the truth not to show our superiority in learning, nor any self-righteousness on our part, nor because we get a carnal thrill out of cornering someone with the truth. It means loving the one in error while seeking to instruct him more perfectly in the way of the Lord. It means hating the sin and trying to rescue the sinner. It means that although we are soldiers of the cross, fighting the good fight of faith, wielding the sword of the Spirit, we are soldiers whose armor of God covers lives which are trying to embody the qualities of love. (Eph. 6:10-18; 1 Cor. 13)

On the óther hand, it must be remembered that it is *truth* which we are to speak in love. Devotion to truth involves opposition to error. The more serious the error the more necessary and determined the opposition. Love is not an emotionalism which refuses to teach truth because it might hurt someone's feelings. Do you want a doctor who refuses to operate because it might hurt your feelings?

While love speaks truth, love studies and seeks for the best way to speak the truth to an indivdiual or a given group of individuals.

It is not easy, but we must try to grow in the grace of combining the spirit of the combatant against sin and error with the spirit of the lover of the sinner. We are helped tremendously in this when we start realizing more fully that it is because of love for God, Christ, the Spirit, the truth, and mankind, that we fight the good fight of faith against foes within and without. This enables us to grow out of the spirit of hostility into the spirit of helpfulness.

THE WALLS OF GOD

Second, the Bible shows that there are walls which God has erected. There is the wall between the church and the world. There is the wall of the Lord's teaching against denominationalism. There is the wall between the church and those from whom it has been necessary to withdraw, or who have withdrawn from us. Love which is helpful must oppose sin and error. Love must not tear down any walls God has erected.

The walls, however, which God has erected are not walls which shut us out from communication, and association on certain levels, with others. Through the wall of truth we must reach out with hands of helpfulness to men in error, just as we want them to try to help us with errors in which we are involved. We must not demolish the wall between the church and the world, and destroy the church; but we must love the world, for God so loved the world that in Christ He came to the world and Christ died for mankind. (John 3:16; Rom. 5:6-10) Although the disfellowshiped was not to be companied with in certain ways, "count him not as an enemy, but admonish him as a brother." (2 Thess. 3:14-15) The walls of God are not designed to keep love flowing from one heart to another.

These walls do not mean that we cannot associate with people with whom we are in even radical disagreements concerning truth. Although, as in everything else, we shall make mistakes, we should seek opportunities to establish contact with others; to learn from them (even the Pharisees when in Moses seat taught truth which was to be heeded, Matt. 23:1-4; compare Phil. 1:15-18) as well as to instruct them. Obviously, this does not mean that any truth which we hold is to be sacrificed.

Although we should not try to tumble down any walls which God has erected we have to tumble down, at one time or another, some which men have erected.

CONTACT TO COMPROMISE

Third, it is possible to let one's feelings lead from contact to compromise. There are some who are hostile to others, and when they make contact with them they find that they have many fine qualities, and are very likeable individuals. One may swing from personal hostility to such a warm friendship that he hesitates to teach the other individual. True friendship, however, wants to share truth and we should look for opportunities to share. We should not expect others to have horns just because they differ with us and we with them. We do not have to have horns to differ, so why should they have to grow them? The author has had warm friendships with agnostics, modernists, and Roman Catholics; as well as an appreciation for a Moslem whom he knows, as well as people who are adherents of other world religions.

Mr. du Plessis, having decided he should establish contact with others, was naturally led to seek those who were the most opposed in beliefs to his, i.e., to the modernist World Council of Churches. He then recites some things which he was convinced were divine guidance which were involved in his contact with the Council, and the many contacts which followed. In his discussion with the Episcopal priest, who asked him whether he thought Pentecostals have the truth and the other churches do not, the context is that of his association with modernists or liberals. In this context he said: "We both have the truth." Other churches had *the same truth;* the basic difference was in the ways of handling it. The other churches had it "on ice, we have ours on fire." He thought he was guided by God into this answer. (pp. 58-59)

As a matter of fact, this is sufficient proof that, regardless of whether or not one can explain all the events in du Plessis' claim of guidance, the Spirit, who is the Spirit of truth, did not guide him into an acknowledgment of false doctrine. Where is the sameness, where is the identity, of truth in such positions as (a) The inspiration of the Bible as affirmed by Pentecostals and denied by modernists? (b) The doctrine of salvation through the atoning death of Christ, and the modernist denial? (c) Faith in the bodily resurrection of Christ, and the denial of it. These are only some of the "same truths" shared by Pentecostals and the people who control the World Council, many of the seminaries, and many of the top positions in a wide variety of denominations.

How could the Spirit lead anyone to the conclusion that "we both have the same truth" — that is the Pentecostals, the other churches, and du Plessis thinks that it covers the New Testament also for he thinks he is an adherent of primitive Christianity. The Spirit does not teach there are many bodies, many faiths, many hopes, and many baptisms. The Spirit does not teach conflicting doctrines about the nature of Christ, who is the revelation of the Father. The Holy Spirit, the one Spirit, does not speak with conflicting voices. (Eph. 4:1-6)

Contacts which we allow to develop into compromise — and we realize that some people view as compromise things which are not really compromises — are not the type of developments in which Christians should engage. We must have contact with others, but not at the expense of truth.

BE YE SEPARATE

We are not to separate ourselves from others through hate,

A REVIEW OF "THEY SPEAK WITH OTHER TONGUES"

through laziness, through self-righteousness, etc. Others are not to be separate from our love. Although it takes some thought to keep from misapplying scriptures such as follow, God was not speaking in vain nor in compromise when He said through Paul: "Be not unequally yoked with unbelievers: for what fellowship have righteousness and iniquity? or what communion hath light with darkness? And what concord hath Christ with Belial? or what portion hath a believer with an unbeliever? And what agreement hath a temple of God with idols? for we are a temple of the living God; even as God said, I will dwell in them, and walk in them; and I will be their God, and they shall be my people. Wherefore

"Come ye out from among them, and be ye separate, saith the Lord, and touch no unclean thing; and I will receive you. And will be to you a Father, and ye shall be to me sons and daughters, saith the Lord Almighty.

"Having therefore these promises, beloved, let us cleanse ourselves from all defilement of flesh and spirit, perfecting holiness in the fear of God." (2 Cor. 6:14; 7:1)

Not every type of yoking is an *unequal* yoke with unbelievers, not every type of contact is a fellowshipping of iniquity, and not every type of communication is a communion of light with darkness, and every type of concord with an unbeliever is not a concord between Christ and Belial. *But* there are contacts which people have allowed to develop into the things which are condemned in Paul's statement. There are walls which men have allowed to crumble down, or which they actively tumble down, which God has erected to enable His people to be separate in the sense in which He has ordained separation.

Regardless of what signs, or claims of signs, an individual has, we must go to the law and to the testimony. (Isa. 8:20) All experiences and doctrines must be measured by the word of God. It is possible to claim, and to convince oneself that he has done miraculous things, and yet not to have done the will of God. (Matt. 7:21-23) It is also possible to refute the claims of Pentecostals, and at the same time fail to live and to speak the truth in love and therefore fail to do the will of God.

SEEKING THE BAPTISM OF THE SPIRIT

In *They Speak With Other Tongues,* John L. Sherrill gives a brief historical survey of the beginnings in modern times of what some call baptism in the Spirit and speaking with tongues. It is doubtful that one can find the very first instance, which Sherrill searched for, "of someone's speaking in tongues in modern times."

(p. 33) There are those who deny that it ever completely died out. There are others who affirm that it did. Some think the first case took place in connection with the seekers in the school of Charles F. Parham in Topeka, Kansas. "The Pentecostals look back on this hour — 7:00 p.m., New Year's Eve, 1900 — as one of the key dates in their history. They point to it as the first time since the days of the early Church that the Baptism in the Holy Spirit had been sought, where speaking in tongues was expected as the initial evidence." (p. 38) Those who believe that tongues ceased, and then started again, should remember that Paul said that *tongues would cease.* (1 Cor. 13:8) He did not teach they would start again long after they had ceased.

THEY WERE LEFT IN DENOMINATIONALISM

Charles Parham was one of the founders of at least part of the Pentecostal movement. Presbyterians in Armenia, Baptists in North Carolina, Anglicans in India, and Methodists in Chile became involved. All of these either continued in their own denomination or joined a Pentecostal denomination. (pp. 33, 44-50) How could this be the work of the Holy Spirit? The Holy Spirit in the first century brought people into the body of Christ which is not a denomination, taught that there is one body (1 Cor. 1:10-13; Eph. 4:1-6), taught that denominationalism (even in its very beginnings) is contrary to the will of God, and revealed and confirmed truth; not truth plus false doctrines.

When this type of argument was presented to one of our brethren, whose book is scheduled to be published awhile later, his reply was that the Holy Spirit was working in these people in various denominations and would gradually unite them in the one church. To this we say: *First,* in His word the Holy Spirit has already told us that denominationalism is wrong. *Second,* the Spirit has already revealed what we must do to be saved, in what body or church God has placed the saved, and what we must do to remain saved. Why don't these people hear the voice of the Spirit in the Bible on these subjects? Surely if they are inspired by the Spirit, if they have the miraculous gifts of the Spirit, the Spirit in them would either reveal these things to them directly or tell them to read these things in the Bible. But these people continue in denominationalism, they continue to teach some false doctrine, and they think that their positions are confirmed by the gifts which they think they have. *Third,* why is it taking so long for the Spirit to reveal these things to these people today which He has already revealed in the first century? It did not take Paul long to tell the Corinthians that division was wrong. (1 Cor.

1:10-13) Many decades, in fact a century or more, have passed since people in this country claimed such miraculous manifestations of the Spirit. In the 1830s Joseph Smith, Jr. and his followers claimed all of the gifts, including the gift of apostleship and the power to write inspired scriptures.

SEEKING THE BAPTISM AND TONGUES

Because he felt his life and ministry were without power, a Methodist minister, Charles F. Parham, started a school in Topeka, Kansas in which he and his students studied the scriptures and sought the baptism of the Holy Spirit. They became convinced that to receive it one had to have hands laid on one, and he also had to speak in tongues as the evidence that he had received the baptism. Finally on New Year's Eve, 1900 the first case took place, and it was followed by others. Let us briefly compare their experience with the New Testament.

They accepted, and acted, on the idea that one must seek — and that constantly if necessary — the baptism. (pp. 35-36) There is no place in the Scriptures where men were told to seek for the baptism in the Holy Spirit. The apostles were not seeking the baptism, but waiting for Christ to fulfill His specific promise that not many days hence they would be baptized in the Spirit. They were *not seeking*. They were *waiting* until Jesus did what He promised He would do — send the Spirit to endow them with power. (Acts 1:5-8; 2:1-4; 33)

The household of Cornelius was not instructed to seek the Spirit. They were not told about the baptism of the Holy Spirit. They were not expecting the baptism. Christ sent the Spirit, without even notifying them beforehand, as Peter began to speak. (Acts 10:44-47; 11:15)

Although the author does not agree with Parham, Parham thought that the following were also cases of baptism in the Spirit. (a) The Samaritans. These were not seeking baptism in the Spirit. The apostles conferred the Spirit, with miraculous manifestations, through the laying on of their hands. (Acts 8:14-19) (b) Saul at Damascus. (Acts 9:19) However, Saul did not receive baptism in the Spirit through the laying on of Ananias' hands. Ananias laid on hands that Saul might receive his sight. (Acts 9:19) Saul's receiving the Spirit was contingent on Ananias' coming, but Ananias did not say he laid hands on Saul for that purpose. (Acts 9:17) Saul's reception of the indwelling of the Spirit was contingent on Ananias' coming and baptising him into Christ. (Acts 9:18; 22:16; 2:38) The baptism Saul received when Ananias came was water baptism. (Matt. 28:19; Acts 8:37; Acts 9:18; 22:16)

Saul was praying, but he was not told to seek, nor was he then seeking, the baptism of the Spirit. (c) The disciples in Ephesus were not told they would be baptized in the Spirit, nor were they seeking such a baptism. Paul did confer the Spirit on them in a miraculous way through the laying on of his hands. (Acts 19:1-7) No one was ever *commanded* to be baptized in the Spirit, no one was ever told *what he must do* in order to be baptized in the Spirit, and no one in the New Testament was told *to seek* the baptism in the Spirit. Is it not a different "Spirit" today which tells these people to seek baptism in the Spirit?

THE BAPTISM WHICH IS COMMANDED

Baptism is commanded in the great commission, and it is for all believing penitents. (Matt. 28:19) There is but one baptism required of men under the new covenant. It involves the water and Spirit, and is the baptism which the Spirit has commanded: water baptism into Christ. Therefore, Philip, working by the inspiration of the Spirit under the great commission, baptized the Eunuch in water. (John 3:2-5; Acts 8:36) Saul could have received baptism of the Spirit while on his knees, but he had to arise and be baptized. (Acts 9:18; 22:16) Peter commanded the household of Cornelius to obey in water baptism. (Acts 10:47-48) This is the one baptism required of men under the new covenant. (Eph. 4:1-6)

It is more than strange, it is inexplicable, that the Spirit instructed the people on Pentecost to be baptized (Acts 2:38), the Samaritans were baptized (Acts 8:12-13), Saul was baptized (9:18; 22:16), Cornelius' household (10:47-48), and the Ephesians were baptized (Acts 19:1-7); *but the "Spirit" that these people receive, with tongues and revelations, does not instruct them to be baptized into Christ immediately.* Some claim that since they have been baptized in the Spirit they do not need water baptism. Peter pointed out that the baptism in the Spirit which the household of Cornelius received was positive proof that they were to be baptized. (Acts 10:47-48) These people today are not being guided in their teaching by the same Spirit who guided the apostles and prophets in the New Testament.

Why do these people seek the baptism in the Spirit, which was never commanded, and fail as a general rule to seek the water baptism which is commanded in the Bible?

ADMINISTERED BY CHRIST, NOT BY MEN

The baptism in the Spirit on Pentecost was administered by Christ, directly from heaven, without human hands; and this is

A REVIEW OF "THEY SPEAK WITH OTHER TONGUES"

also true of the case of Cornelius. (Acts 1:5-8; 10:44-48) Ananias did not lay hands on Saul to baptize him in the Spirit. The only imparting of the Spirit, in miraculous manifestations, through human hands was done through the hands of the apostles. (Acts 8:14, 17-18; Acts 19:6) Parham, who was not an apostle, and did not even claim to be baptized in the Spirit, laid hands on the first one in his group who supposedly was then baptized in the Spirit. (p. 38)

REVEALED AND CONFIRMED TRUTH

The apostles were enabled by the baptism of the Spirit to begin their work, with power, of revealing and confirming the truth. (Acts 1:8) They revealed truth, not error, and by going through Acts one can see the wide variety of miracles which they wrought. At the household of Cornelius the baptism of the Holy Spirit, with the accompanying revelations, revealed and confirmed the truth that the gospel was for Gentiles as well as Jews; and Gentiles did not have to have anything to do with the law of Moses. (Acts 15:7-12)

Pentecostals teach a wide variety of errors, they are not inspired, they do not write scriptures, and they do not match the miracles of the Bible.

TONGUES

On Pentecost the apostles spoke in human languages and all understood. The apostle Peter and the six Jews with him understood the praises Cornelius gave to God in tongues. (Acts 2:4, 6, 8, 11; 10:47-48) The woman on whom Parham laid hands spoke syllables "which neither one of them could understand." (p. 38) The tongues like as of fire, and the mighty wind, were also missing in Topeka, Kansas. (Compare Acts 2:1-4)

Later on others, in their prayer room in the presence of others, got the gift of "tongues," and violated 1 Cor. 14:2-6, 27-28, by speaking in tongues which those present did not understand.

In connection with another group—which grew out of the Parham work—in California it was claimed that a girl spoke in Hebrew and identified a stranger and converted him. (pp. 42-43) The author does not know enough about this case to check on it, but he does not believe it was the work of the Holy Spirit. *First,* this girl got up in a prayer meeting and spoke to the Jew who came into the meeting. Why was a woman speaking in tongues in such a public prayer meeting? The Holy Spirit said: "As in all the churches of the saints, let the women keep silence in the churches: for it is not permitted unto them to speak; but let them be in subjection, as also saith the law." (1 Cor. 14:33-34) Surely the Spirit did not inspire her to violate the teaching of the Spirit. Perhaps Paul was wrong, some may say. Paul said: "If any man thinketh himself to be a prophet, or spiritual, let him take knowledge of these things which I write unto you, that they are the commandment of the Lord." (1 Cor. 14:37) *Second,* although we do not know all the doctrines held by this young woman, we are convinced there are other places where she contradicted the Bible.

Since we are to be judged by Christ's word (John 12:48), we must measure all movements, experiences, and teachings in the light of the Bible which contains the faith once for all delivered unto the saints. (Jude 3) The author is convinced that the evidences show that whatever may be the explanation of the experiences of these people, it is not the work of the Holy Spirit who revealed and confirmed the New Testament, and who speaks to us through the New Testament.

EVIDENCES OF BAPTISM IN THE SPIRIT?

What, according to some of the tongues speakers, constitutes proof that one has received the miraculous baptism in the Holy Spirit? *First,* there is no agreement among all tongues speakers on what constitutes proof. Some justify their divergence, although they claim to all have the same Spirit, by saying that the Spirit is unpredictable and therefore the results of baptism in the Spirit are unpredictable. We shall examine this in another chapter. On the other hand, there are those who say that they know how the Spirit proves His presence. It is always through the gift of tongues. *Second,* while some of them claim scriptures to justify their arguments and experiences, there are others who do not claim scripture. If the Spirit is unpredictable, one would not always be able to furnish scriptural justification for his positions and experiences.

SOME PROOFS

First, some maintain that it is an inward conviction without an outward sign.

Second, some say that tongues are the proof.

Third, one said that it "felt like receiving a massive jolt of electricity, painless but stimulating." (John L. Sherrill, *They Speak With Other Tongues,* p. 112) This is a shocking experience for which there is no scripture! How one distinguishes this from touching a live wire, we do not know; unless the wire has too much voltage. Under certain conditions some people give one an electric shock when they touch them.

Fourth, "Sometimes these jolts of power produce physical

manifestations. A person's muscles may react, flexing and relaxing until he begins to shake all over. Or he may start to cry, or sing. Or he may literally be prostrated: the Holy Rollers, who are for the most part Negro Pentecostals, get their name from this unusual manifestation." (p. 112) Where are the scriptures for these proofs? Is God the God of such confusion as among the "Holy Rollers"? (1 Cor. 14:33) Some dance, some laugh, some are drunk with joy, some claim to be healed, and some claim peace. (113)

Fifth, some claim they now feel the presence of Jesus.

PRESENCE OF JESUS

It is maintained that with the baptism of the Holy Spirit they are drawn closer to Jesus so that he is a personal presence rather than just a character in a book. "His Spirit was with the baptized believer in a present-time, minute-by-minute way, showing him at every turn the nature and personality of Christ."

Sherrill thought he had seen Jesus when he saw an unusual light when he was sick in the hospital. He wanted Christ to return, and finally concluded that He comes to one again in the baptism of the Spirit. "Wasn't the lesson I had learned from the Bible, and from the people who had had the experience today, that in order to see Him again we need the mediation of the Holy Spirit? 'But when your Advocate has come, whom I will send you from the Father — the Spirit of truth that issues from the Father — he will bear witness to me.'" (John 15:26. Sherrill, p. 115)

In a previous chapter we have given reasons for rejecting Sherrill's interpretation of the light-experience as being an appearance of Jesus Christ. At this time we shall point out why we are convinced he has misunderstood John 15:26. *First,* Jesus was talking to the apostles. (Matt. 26:20-25; John 13:1-30; 17:6-12) *Second,* although in the conversation with the apostles Jesus did set forth some principles, and although we benefit from the fulfillment of His promises to them, there were certain promises which were made to the apostles and not to us. (a) "These things have I spoken unto you, while yet abiding with you. But the Comforter, even the Holy Spirit, whom the Father will send in my name, he shall teach you all things, and bring to your remembrance all that I said unto you." (John 14:25-26) We were not with Him in His personal ministry. We were not taught by Him personally. We do not learn what Jesus taught in His personal ministry, by direct inspiration. Who among us today knows anything about what Jesus taught in His personal ministry unless he learned it from the four Gospels or from someone who learned it from the four Gospels? If this promise is to us, we have an inspired remembrance of all that Jesus taught. We say, without fear of successful contradiction, that no one today learned the four Gospels through personal association with Christ and, that to keep him from forgetting, the Spirit now inspires him with a remembrance of all Jesus taught.

(b) We should not only quote John 15:26 but also the next verse which is a part of the same sentence. "But when the Comforter is come, whom I will send unto you from the Father, even the Spirit of truth, which proceedeth from the Father, he shall bear witness of me: *and ye also* bear witness, because ye have been with me from the beginning." (John 15:26-27) *We do not bear witness of Him because we have been with Jesus from the beginning.* Who today was with Him in His personal ministry? Who, as an eye witness, can bear testimony to what took place in the personal ministry? After Christ ascended, and began His reign, He sent the Spirit with all the miraculous manifestations which took place on Pentecost. (Acts 2:4, 6, 8, 11, 33) Those who obeyed the gospel continued stedfastly in the apostles' doctrine. (Acts 2:42) Mr. Sherrill didn't get the Spirit as did the apostles on Pentecost, as far as we know he does not claim to have spoken in languages which others understood but which he had not learned, as far as we know he has not understood or obeyed Acts 2:38, and as far as we know he does not claim that we should continue stedfastly in Sherrill's doctrine just as we do the apostles' doctrine. If this promise applies to him, as it did to the apostles, his word is just as authoritative as that of the apostles.

(c) If John 15:26 applies to Sherrill, so does John 16:7-13. Jesus again mentioned His promise to send the Spirit after He went away. (John 16:7) The Spirit, Jesus said, would convict the world of sin, righteousness, and judgment. The Spirit would guide them into all the truth. Has Sherrill been guided into all the truth, or is he in the process of being guided into all the truth, by the direct inspiration of the Spirit? Furthermore, Jesus said that the Spirit would convict the world of sin, righteousness, and judgment. To know how the Spirit did this, through the word of truth which He revealed and confirmed, we turn to Acts 2 where Jesus' promise began to be fulfilled. Jesus sent the Spirit. (Acts 2:1-4, 33) People were convinced they had sinned in rejecting Christ. They recognized that He was that righteous one and that they were unrighteous. They realized that He now rules and has power to bring all His enemies, including the devil, into subjection. (Acts 2:34-36) These people were convicted of sin, righteousness, and judgment. Therefore, they wanted to know what to do. They were concerned as to what they could do about their sinful condition for, in answering their question, Peter told them what to do about their sins. He said: "Repent ye, and be baptized every one of you in the name of Jesus Christ unto the remission of your sins; and ye shall receive the gift of the Holy Spirit." (Acts 2:38) The apostles then exhorted them to do it, all who gladly received the word were baptized, and they continued stedfastly in the apostles' doctrine, fellowship, the breaking of bread and the prayers. (Acts 2:40-42) When the Spirit supposedly came on Sherrill, did he teach sinners what the apostles taught them? Does he teach the same doctrine concerning the nature of baptism (immersion — burial and resurrection), who can be baptized (believers), the purpose or purposes of baptism (into Christ, unto the remission of sins, etc.), and is what he teaches them, to continue in, the apostles' doctrine or does it contain some of the traditions of men? If Sherrill received the same Spirit in fulfillment of the same promises Jesus made to the apostles, he would teach what the Spirit taught through the apostles. However, on some of these subjects he teaches the traditions of men.

(d) Jesus also said: "I have yet many things to say unto you, but ye cannot bear them now. Howbeit when he, the Spirit of truth, is come, he shall guide you into all the truth: for he shall not speak from himself; but what things soever he shall hear, these shall he speak: and he shall declare unto you the things that are to come. He shall glorify me: for he shall take of mine, and shall declare it unto you." (John 16:12-14) What did Jesus teach Sherrill in the personal ministry? What things did He refrain from teaching Sherrill because he could not then bear them? When did the Spirit by direct inspiration teach Sherrill these unbearable things which were not taught him in the personal ministry? Is the Spirit guiding Sherrill, by direct inspiration, into all the truth? If the Spirit was guiding him into all the truth, if Sherrill had minute-by-minute guidance of the Spirit "showing him at every turn the nature and personality of Christ," why did the Spirit allow him to misunderstand John 15:26 and some other passages of Scripture? This certainly was not a part of the process of guiding him into all the truth. Since Jesus' promise had to be fulfilled in the lifetime of the apostles, by the time the last apostle died all the truth had been delivered; or Jesus' promise failed. The Spirit today would not make revelations in addition to the ones in the Bible. He would not make revelations contrary to the New Testament. What things to come, comparable with that which was revealed to the apostles in the New Testament, were revealed to Sherrill? Furthermore, the Spirit came to glorify *Christ,* and not Himself. Study from Acts through Revelation and see how He glorifies Christ.

Third, what shall we say about their conviction that they experience the personal presence of Jesus? (a) Christ has promised to be with His people, but we do not see Him. "Whom not having seen ye love; on whom, though now ye see him not, yet believing, ye rejoice greatly with joy unspeakable and full of glory." (1 Pet. 1:8) (b) By faith we should perceive His presence for Paul said "that Christ may dwell in your hearts through faith." (Eph. 3:17) We do not always remember that we live our lives in the presence of Jesus, but it is a fact and we need to keep it in remembrance. However, even those like Sherrill, who think they have seen the Lord, are not always conscious of His presence. (*They Speak With Other Tongues,* pp. 15-16, 121-122, 127-128) It is no reflection, therefore, on our faith if we uninspired disciples are not always keenly aware of His presence. It is just a fact of life that we cannot concentrate on one thing all of the time. If we tried always to fix our minds on the presence of Christ, we would not have time to give attention to the presence of other people. However, we should live by the conviction that our lives are lived in His presence and we should conduct ourselves accordingly. But this does not mean that we always have an intense awareness of His presence. (c) As one believes, so at least at times one feels. If one believes that he has been miraculously baptized in the Spirit, and that this means the presence of Jesus in an unusual sense, at times, at least, he will feel that Jesus is unusually near him. Jacob believed his son Joseph was dead, but his intense sorrow did not mean that his son was dead. Because these people feel that Jesus is present in a miraculous baptism of the Spirit, does not mean that they have actually been miraculously baptized in the Spirit.

We do not believe that the evidences of the miraculous baptism of the Spirit, which Sherrill mentioned as the beliefs of some of the Pentecostals, are proofs that they have been baptized in the Spirit. When their claims are evaluated in the light of the Bible, we believe their claims are unsustained.

WITNESSES AND POWER

In arguing for the baptism of the Holy Spirit, tongues, and other miracles today, John L. Sherrill spoke both of the power and of the witnessing done by those who had received the baptism. He quoted Jesus' statement that: "ye shall receive power, when the Holy Spirit is come upon you: and ye shall be my witnesses both in Jerusalem, and in all Judaea and Samaria, and unto the uttermost part of the earth." (Acts 1:8) (Sherrill, 138) Jesus was speaking to the apostles concerning their baptism in the Spirit not many days hence. (Acts 1:2-5) The baptism in the Spirit gave them power but it did not in itself qualify them to be witnesses. Christ had done this by being with them in His personal ministry, and after His resurrection. In speaking to the apostles (Matt. 26:20-25; John 13), Jesus said: The Spirit "shall bear witness of me: and *ye also bear witness, because ye have been with me from the beginning.*" (John 15:26-27) ". . . the apostles whom he had chosen: to whom he also showed himself alive after his passion by many proofs, appearing unto them by the space of forty days. . . ." (Acts 1:2-3) To have been with Him, and to have seen Him after His resurrection, were essential. However, in addition to this, a person had to be selected by Christ to be an apostle and witness. Therefore, although two others had been with Christ only one was selected to be a witness to the resurrected Christ and to take the place of Judas. Peter said: "Of the men therefore that have companied with us all the time that the Lord Jesus went in and went out among us, beginning from the baptism of John, unto the day that he was received up from us, of these must *one become a witness* with us of his resurrection." (Acts 1:21-22) Matthias was chosen. He was one of the apostles who bore witness on Pentecost to the resurrected Christ. (Acts 2:14, 32; 6:2) One does not have to be miraculously guided by the Spirit in order to know that we cannot be witnesses such as those mentioned in Acts 1:8. Although Saul had not been with Jesus in His personal ministry, yet he, too, had to see the resurrected Lord. (1 Cor. 15:8-9; 22:14-15; 26:16) One certainly is not being guided by the Spirit when he applies Acts 1:8 to himself.

MIRACULOUS POWER

Although there were others who received miraculous power, the apostles were promised miraculous power in Acts 1:8. Jesus said they would receive "power, when the Holy Spirit is come upon you." (Acts 1:8) What power did they receive, and what miracles did they work? They received power to work miracles. (Acts 2:43; 4:33; 5:12) What were some of the miracles which they wrought, as well as those worked by others who later received power? (1) They spoke in other languages. (2:4, 6, 8, 11) This was in the setting of the tongues like as of fire which sat upon each of them, and the sound as of a rushing mighty wind. (2:2-4, 33) (2) Instantaneous, undeniable, public, complete healing of the lame man. (3:2, 6, 7-9, 16; 4:9, 14, 22) (3) Place shaken. (4:31) (4) Peter predicted the death of Sapphira and she died immediately. (5:9-10) (5) All the sick who were brought to them were healed. (5:15-17) (6) Miraculous, instantaneous deliverance from prison. (5:18-19; 12:7-11) (7) Cast out unclean spirits. (8:7; 16:16, 18) (8) Palsied healed. (8:7; 9:33-34) (9) Lame healed. (8:7) (10) Apostles conferred the Spirit, with miraculous manifestations, through the laying on of their hands. (Acts 8:14-20; 19:1-6) (11) Philip caught away. (8:39) (12) Personal appearance of Christ to Saul. (9:17) (13) Dead raised. (9:37-41) (14) Vision of Cornelius corroborated by that of Peter, and confirmed by miraculous baptism in the Spirit. (Acts 10) (15) Paul prophesied the immediate blindness of Elymas. (13:8-12) (16) Life-long cripple. (14:8-10) (17) Although left for dead, Paul rose up. (14:19-20) (18) Earthquake which loosed the bands and opened the doors of the prison, but no one escaped. (16:26-28) (19) Healed through handkerchiefs or aprons. (19:11-12) (20) Evil spirit acknowledged that he knew who Jesus and Paul were. (19:13-16) (21) Eutychus restored after his fall. (20:9-10) (22) Paul knew of the consequences of a voyage. (27:9-11, 21) (23) Paul knew that none would be harmed, if they hearkened to his word, but they would be cast on an island. (27:21-26) (24) Paul not hurt by viper bite. (28:3-6) (25) Publius' father healed of fever and dysentery. (28:8) (26) All cured who were brought to Paul. (28:9)

One should compare and contrast the characteristics of the healing miracles of Christ and the apostles with those of so-called modern healers.

One should compare and contrast the wide variety of miracles of Christ, the apostles and prophets, with the limited variety of "miracles" of the so-called modern miracle workers. Among other things, do they walk on the water, multiply the loaves and the fishes, and do they always succeed in working miracles or do they try and fail? After the apostles received the baptism of the Spirit, there is no case where they tried and failed.

We must also ask whether they write inspired scripture, as did the apostles and prophets, and whether their teaching harmonizes with the New Testament.

MIRACLE?

One person prayed for a child injured in an accident, and with conviction told the mother the child would get well. (Sherrill,

85-86) *First,* have they ever had such a conviction and the person did not get well? *Second,* one could have this conviction and be right sometimes without it being a miracle. *Third,* the girl gradually got better. Twelve weeks later she was back in school with only some "hair-fine scars on" her "face and arms." This was not a miracle, it was not an instantaneous act which gave her perfect soundness.

MOVED

There are cases where people feel moved to do something, and it turns out it was the right thing for them to do. Is this supernatural? *First,* the author does not believe it is supernatural. There is no superhuman demonstration of power, which even the unbeliever can see is supernatural. *Second,* all of us have had such things happen to us. We should be grateful that we did act in such cases. How God may work in His providence, how He may work behind the scenes, to accomplish His purposes, is one of the unrevealed things which we leave to God. (Deut. 29:29) *Third,* there are cases where people have had an intuition to do something, and it worked out, but it was not an answer to prayer and the person may not have been religious. There are religious people who get impressions at times that someone in their family needs them, and they do. However, they do not view this as an indication that they are inspired or have the power to work miracles. *Fourth,* likely all of us have had an intuition or feeling, have acted on it, and it did not turn out well. We tend to forget these cases. In some casse we may feel something is going to happen, and it does not. We are apt to forget the times when it did not happen, and remember the times when it did happen.

While we may act on hunches and intuitions, at times at least, it would be wrong for us to think that because we have a hunch it is inspired and, therefore, God authorizes us to do thus and so; and anyone who differs with us about it is opposing God. All things must be measured by the word of God.

WHAT IF?

What if some sincere people testify that they have been miraculously healed? It is important to remember that some sincere people have testified that they have been healed when in reality they have not been healed; or it was not a miraculous healing. What shall we say to these testimonies? (a) We do not fully understand the power of the mind over the body. (b) For some reason sometimes a certain bodily process has reversed itself, or stopped, and people have recovered from what otherwise would have killed them. There was no supernatural recovery with the characteristics of the healing miracles of Jesus; but over a period of time they recovered. We do not know enough about the human body, and all its processes, to understand fully the power of the body and of the mind. (c) They may have been so emotionally and psychologically stimulated that they temporarily ignore the sickness. (d) Their illness may be internal. They feel better at the moment, so they think that they are healed. (e) They ignore the distinction between a slow natural recovery and a miraculous recovery. Thus because they are gradually feeling better, and actually gradually getting better, they think that a "healer" has miraculously healed them. But how could this be a miracle, a manifestation of supernatural power, if it is just like the natural recovery? How can it be a sign, when it does not differ from other cases where the people have gradually gotten well without the "healer's" help? (f) Mental attitude does have an important relationship to getting well in many, many cases of illness. (g) Some are deceived by healers into believing the following: Claim the healing in faith and you are healed. If you claim it in faith, you have it! Since you have it, in gratitude — as well as to help others — to God you should testify and thus glorify God, giving Him the credit. You still have the symptoms? The devil put them there to shake your faith in your healing. Are you going to believe God or the devil? If you believe God, testify. If you believe the devil, and conclude that you have not been healed, you will lose your healing! (see Mrs. Fitch, *The Healing Delusion*) (h) There are also, of course, conscious deceivers. (i) Some just thought they were sick. (j) What do they more than others who contradict their teaching?

If an individual performs successful signs, but teaches contrary to the Scriptures (and all the so-called modern miracle workers whom we have tested have contradicted the Bible at one time or another) we would have to reject them and say that if what they did was supernatural it was done by the power of the devil. (2 Thess. 2:9; compare Deut. 13:1-5)

We do not believe there is sufficient evidence to show that Sherrill rightly interpreted Acts 1:8 or that the Pentecostals, and others of their type of persuasion, do the mighty works which are recorded in the Bible.

SHERRILL AND TONGUES

Sherrill thought he received the baptism in the Spirit and the gift of tongues. Those who supposedly receive this baptism are

A REVIEW OF "THEY SPEAK WITH OTHER TONGUES" 97

not agreed on how they know they have received it. What are some of Sherrill's ideas on the baptism of the Spirit and tongues?

There are some who seek the gift of tongues as proof they have been baptized in the Spirit (Sherrill, 79), while others say that the Holy Spirit, Himself, is the only evidence "needed or wanted." (p. 81) Yet both groups are supposed to be miraculously guided by the Spirit.

REVERSAL

There are some who say they would never do thus and so, and yet when convinced concerning tongues and the baptism of the Spirit, they do these things. For example, John L. Sherrill said that the one thing he would never do was to "stand up, raise both hands toward heaven, and shout 'Praise the Lord!'" Of course, when he got the "baptism of the Spirit" he did what he had said he would not do. (pp. 116, 123) These reversals are not hard to explain. Such people become convinced that it is God's will that they do thus and so, that they have not yielded themselves to God unless they go all the way, and that just as a matter of "sheer obedience," if for no other reason, it is necessary for them to do it. Therefore, they do it. It is nothing supernatural, but something which naturally flows from their conviction that if they do not do it they are holding out on God. We wonder how many of them are willing to abandon denominationalism, accept the New Testament teaching on baptism, the church, etc. and become just Christians?

PHYSICAL STRENGTH

There are those who maintain that tongues not only gave them new ability to praise and pray, but also resiliency and physical power to meet life's daily tasks. "This added physical strength and resiliency was another purpose of tongues noted by St. Paul. The man who speaks in tongues, Paul wrote, edifies himself, or builds himself up." (Sherrill, 82; 1 Cor. 14:4) Is this what Paul said? *First,* if it is, when someone speaks in tongues and it is interpreted to the church, the church is built up physically. (1 Cor. 14:5, 26-28) *Second,* the one who prophesies builds up the church physically. ". . . he that prophesieth edifieth the church." (1 Cor. 14:4) *Third,* the edification of which Paul speaks is spiritual edification through the impartation of knowledge, through exhortation, consolation, or teaching, or such like. (1 Cor. 14:4-6) The person is not edified when he does not understand. (14:16-17) Therefore, Paul spoke so as to instruct others. (14:18-19) *Fourth,* if Sherrill, or any of those who advised him, had miraculous guidance of the Spirit, he should have a better understanding of the scriptures than to so misapply 1 Cor. 14:4.

COMPENSATE FOR INADEQUACIES?

Of David Wilkerson, Sherrill wrote: "English could no longer express what he felt. It was simply inadequate for the Being that he perceived." (pp. 82-83) Some seek and exercise tongues in order to overcome felt inadequacies in their prayer and praise life. (81-82) If these inadequacies are compensated for by God giving one the gift of tongues, why are not all other inadequacies compensated for by miraculous gifts? It is very important that we communicate the gospel to others. All of us are inadequate in varying degrees in both knowledge and methods of approach, as well as ways of putting what we do know. Therefore, all of us should get the gift of inspiration so that we shall know what and how to say things. (Matt. 10:19-20)

In what way was the message, when expressed in tongues, more adequate than in English? Sherrill expressed his disappointment, as a rule, with the stereotyped interpretations of tongues. (p. 87) Why was a general message, like walk in the Lord's way, more adequate when expressed in non-intelligible sounds? Its non-intelligibility keeps *them* from realizing how inadequate they are!!

SOME DISAPPOINTMENTS

There were several things about tongues which disappointed Sherrill. *First,* he was disappointed as a general rule in "the content of the interpretation: more often than not it was a stereotyped exhortation to '. . . stand fast in the latter days. . . .' '. . . walk in the way . . . walk in the way of the Lord. . . .'" Why was this more adequate in a tongue than in English?

Second, "I was bothered, too, that the language used was amost exclusively King James English." To this author this suggests that the interpreters were simply weaving together fragments of scripture as they came to their minds.

Third, "I noticed that there was often no correlation between the length of the message in tongues, and the length of the interpretation." (p. 87) If there is so much packed into the tongue, why does so little come through the interpretation? Why isn't the intrepreter more faithful? Why doesn't he give the full content of the message? This author once heard four words in a tongue and well over a hundred words used in the interpretation!!

Fourth, he was disappointed because in his research he did not personally hear a case where a foreign language was spoken by inspiration. He played around forty examples of tongues on tapes to linguists and they could not identify any of them as a human language. How he overcame this disappointment is dealt with in another chapter. (pp. 102-103)

SOME THINGS WHICH IMPRESSED HIM

First, in one case Sherrill was pondering whether he had made the right decision, and a woman spoke in tongues. The interpreter said: "Do not worry, I am pleased with the stand you have taken. This is difficult for you but will bring much blessing to another." (p. 88) To this we say: (a) The speaker in tongues was "a woman Methodist minister. . . ." If God revealed something in that tongues meeting, surely He would not have left them in the dark as to the fact that denominationalism is unscriptural. If the Spirit spoke to this gathering of people from various denominations, and was speaking to their needs, why was nothing said in this meeting which met their need to see that denominationalism is unscriptural and that they should become members of Christ's church; nothing more, nothing less. (b) Why did not the Spirit rebuke her for being a woman preacher? The New Testament does not sanction women preachers, whether they are Methodist or not. Why did she fail to listen to the Spirit as He spoke through Paul and said that women were to be silent in such assemblies? (1 Cor. 14:33-34) This message was just as much a part of the message from God as was the rest of the instruction in 1 Cor. 14. (14:37) (c) It is not amazing that sooner or later in such meetings that some individual should hear something which did deal with some need which he had. There are countless cases where people, listening to preachers and teachers who did not claim to be inspired, thought that something the preacher said indicated that he knew about their situation or their need. If one keeps teaching some of the principles which are in the Bible, if one keeps giving exhortation and encouragement, he is bound to hit home sooner or later.

Second, another thing which impressed Sherrill was that when a message came he had the inner conviction that it was meant for him. "Here was something I had not read in Paul's letters and could not have guessed: that God might accompany the messages with a corroborating conviction in the hearer." (p. 88) This conviction was no proof that God's hand was in this in a miraculous way. There are people who have had the inward conviction that a preacher knew about their case, and they wondered who told him about it, but the preacher did not know. The inward conviction would come because the instruction fitted one's case, and also because, in Sherrill's case, of his involvement in a tongues meeting. Once one of the author's boys said to his mother in church: "The preacher called my name. What did I do?" The boy's name is Mark. The preacher quoted from Mark and identified the source of his quotation. It hit home to my boy Mark, but Mark missed the mark!

ROMANS 8:26-27

Sherrill cited Romans 8:26-27 to prove that "another use of tongues suggested in the Bible is to let us pray even when with our own minds we have no idea what to ask for in a given situation." (pp. 83-84) The groanings mentioned by Paul are not our groanings, and they are not the gift of tongues. They are unutterable groanings of the Spirit making intercession for us with God. Surely the tongues speakers are not uttering groanings which cannot be uttered.

DOUBTS

At least some of those who get the baptism and tongues have their periods of doubt afterward. They may feel as if they generated the tongues and the Spirit had nothing to do with it. (p. 127) In some cases they are told that after Jesus was baptized, and the Spirit came on Him in the form of a dove, He went into the wilderness and was tempted. There is no indication that Christ was ever tempted to doubt that He had the Spirit, but these people may be told that their temptation will be to doubt whether they have received the Spirit. (p. 128) Those who are convinced they have received it, but become weak in faith, will often overcome the doubt through believing the doubt is of the devil and must be put away through faith in God. Some may reassure themselves by again speaking in tongues as they emotionally struggle with the doubt. Of course, it is difficult to reason with people who may view your arguments from the Bible as temptations of the devil!

THEY SPEAK WITH OTHER TONGUES?

In all of his research he did not personally hear a case where a foreign language was spoken by inspiration. After Sherrill had played around forty examples of tongues, which had been taped, to linguists and none of them had identified any of these as a language of man, a tongues speaker said that his mistake was in trying to "isolate language in them." If he met the Holy Spirit, he would not have this problem any more. (Sherrill, 102-103) Finally, he thought, he got the Spirit and tongues.

It surely was a mistake to try to isolate languages in sounds which signified nothing but the fact that the speaker uttered strange sounds.

In one case he heard of, students spoke "strange sounds", and the preacher said "our students were suddenly speaking in tongues, just as at Pentecost." (Sherrill, 109-110) It does not take the gift of knowledge to know that instead of strange sounds being spoken on Pentecost, languages of men were spoken and understood. (Acts 2:4, 6, 8, 11)

MARK 16:17

The Pentecostals, Sherrill pointed out, "set much store by" Mark 16:17, which Sherrill learned that everybody did not accept as "equally authentic." (p. 73) The author accepts these verses as authentic and genuine. He wonders why, however, that Pentecostals who have the gift of knowledge and of inspiration do not give us an infallible pronouncement on this, and on other textual problems in the Bible. They should confirm their pronouncements with miracles, and their teaching should harmonize with the Bible.

ACTS AND CORINTHIANS DIFFERENT?

Sherrill thought that in the Gospels and Acts "tongues have been treated as a sign of the Holy Spirit's coming. But when I turned to Paul's letters it was obvious that he was looking at them very differently. Paul was discussing tongues not as a one-time outpouring, but as a continuing experience. They were important not only as proof of God's presence, but because their use conferred certain benefits on the Church." (pp. 73-74)

"Pentecostals point out that in these three chapters Paul is discussing tongues as a gift only, not tongues as the initial *sign* of the Baptism in the Holy Spirit. They believe that everyone does speak in tongues, however briefly, at the moment of his Baptism, whether or not he is subsequently given the gift of tongues for use in his daily Christian living." (pp. 75-76)

In our book on the gift of tongues we have discussed in detail whether there is a difference between tongues as a sign and tongues as a gift. Here we briefly call to the reader's attention the following: *First,* they have not proved their case. *Second,* the tongues mentioned in Mark 16:17 were one of the signs which *confirmed* the word which was preached. (Mk. 16:20) Tongues in Corinth were a sign. (1 Cor. 14:22) *Third,* Mark 16:20 briefly summarizes the uses of these gifts by the Corinthians and in Acts of Apostles. The very first case was on Pentecost and enabled the apostles to speak in various human languages which they had not learned. (Acts 2:4, 6, 8, 11) *Fourth,* the assumed difference between tongues on Pentecost and tongues in Corinth vanishes when we realize that some in Corinth were using the gift when no one there understood the particular human language which they were speaking by inspiration. On Pentecost there were people present who understood the languages. *Fifth,* if these people had the miraculous guidance of the Spirit today, they would know there is no difference between the gift of tongues in Corinth and the tongues the Spirit gave the apostles on Pentecost.

Sherrill recognized that the vast majority of cases of tongues today are meaningless sounds to the people who speak them and to the people who listen. "This was obviously the kind of tongues St. Paul was familiar with. 'For one who speaks in a tongue speaks not to men . . . for no one understands him. . . .' (1 Cor. 14:2) 'Unknown tongues' was the name often given in the Bible to this phenomenon, and is still the kind most frequently encountered today." (Sherrill, 91) *First,* Paul's statement does not mean that tongues were not human languages. No one understood for the simple reason that no one there knew the language. People were unlearned, and the context shows that Paul is speaking about being unlearned in the language. (14:16) Furthermore, no one understood because no interpreter was present. (14:2, 27-28) *Second,* it does not necessitate any gifts of the Spirit for one to know that the Bible does not call these tongues *unknown* tongues. The word *unknown* is not in the Greek, and it is italicized in the King James in order to let the reader know that this word has been supplied by the translators. Furthermore, the tongues were unknown not because they were non-human languages but because no human beings there understood the particular human languages which were being spoken. We have dealt with this in detail in our book on the gift of tongues.

CASES OF WHICH HE HEARD

Sherrill thought that he had found a few cases where individuals spoke in languages which they had not learned. In at least two cases, people thought they heard their names called — one the name of his father. Concerning these cases in general we make the following observations. *First,* in some cases things were going on which are prohibited by the Scriptures. For example, several praying at one time, some in tongues and some in English. (Sherrill, 90-91) Centuries ago the Spirit revealed that this was not to be done. (1 Cor. 14:26-33) *Second,* why are there so very,

very few cases where people even claim that a foreign language was spoken? *Third,* why, in around forty cases where tape recordings of tongues were played by Sherrill to linguists, did he fail to find any of them were human languages? (Sherrill, 100-102) *Fourth,* why have other linguists in attending Pentecostal meetings, or studying tapes, been unable to verify any of them as languages? *Fifth,* New Testament tongues were languages. A tape recording on Pentecost would have shown they spoke in other languages. (Acts 2:4, 6, 8, 11) *Sixth,* it is extremely difficult for individuals — especially in today's world — to keep from hearing at least snatches of foreign languages. Records, radio, TV, motion pictures, and news casts expose one sooner or later to foreign languages. This country has had immigrants from many different countries. One sometimes hears foreign languages as he rides on a train, or subway, or visits some large cities. There have been cases where people, in a highly wrought emotional state, have spoken languages which they had not learned but had heard. These had made an impression on their minds. They could not call forth these sounds at will, but in sickness or in a highly emotional state they have spoken them. Out of the millions of cases of speaking in tongues in this century, the wonder is not that this may have happened in a few instances, but that it has not happened in more of these highly charged emotional services. *Seventh,* in some cases we mis-hear. Out of the millions of cases of tongues, it would be amazing if someone didn't think he heard a language, or his own name, but it was his own interpretation or mis-hearing of sounds. *Eighth,* the tongues speakers teach false doctrine.

Sherrill cited what he believed was a case where a missionary in Africa was being tried, or so he interpreted it, by a tribe which had captured him. After the witch doctor spoke, the actions of the witch doctor and the crowd indicated it was his turn to speak. He prayed for the Spirit's help, shook violently, felt the Spirit was near, remembered Jesus' statement to take no thought as to how or what to say, became bold, and started speaking words which he did not understand. He was thoroughly convinced he spoke their language. Finally "the speech-power" vanished, they let him go, and later the tribe was converted. The missionary did not understand anything which he said. (Sherrill, 90-100) This missionary was very fortunate but there is no proof he spoke in their language by inspiration. *First,* the missionary did not know what he said, and no evidence was given to show that these natives said that he spoke their language. *Second,* a superstitious people hearing a white man, and it was likely they had never seen one before, speaking such strange sounds could be impressed by it whether they understood a word of what he was saying. Witch doctors have spoken in "tongues," and they may have thought that his tongues sounded like some they had heard and, therefore, the man himself was a witch doctor whom they should let go. *Third,* the missionary was involved in this incident as a result of a series of incidents due to the sickness of his wife. It is strange that he did not work a miracle and heal his wife instead of trying to get medicine for her. *Fourth,* if he was inspired by the Spirit in this case, why didn't the Spirit inspire him in some other situations and lead him out of denominationalism?

HARALD BREDESEN

Pat Boone wrote that: "In my search for this dynamic reality, for answers to my urgent needs, for a real, vibrant relationship with Jesus, I studied with several Spirit-filled men whose daily lives radiated joy, power and love. Among these were David Wilkerson, Ralph Wilkerson, George Otis, and Harald Bredesen. It is impossible to be around these men and to deny that God is in their lives, leading, shielding, blessing and using them in mighty ways." (*Testimony,* No. 30, p. 8)

Harald Bredesen, once the pastor of the First Reformed Church, Mt. Vernon, New York (*The Christian Reader,* Dec.-Jan., 1963-64, p. 46), was one of the significant figures in the tongues movement dealt with in John L. Sherrill, *They Speak With Other Tongues.* Bredesen reported that in one case someone told him he had spoken in Polish, and another case an individual said he spoke in old Arabic. (pp. 19, 20) In these two cases, the individual was the only one present.

The author does not know how to check on these cases.

There are, however, linguists who have checked Bredesen's tongues and did not recognize his tongues as human languages. (*Christianity Today,* Sept. 13, 1963) Dr. Eugene A. Nida, a linguist with the American Bible Society, analyzed some tapes of Bredesen's tongues, and his conclusion was that they were not languages. They were ecstatic speech without the essential characteristics of languages of men. (Letter to the author, May 13, 1970) Since tongues were for a sign, confirming the gospel (Mk. 16:17, 20; 1 Cor. 14:22), it is more than strange that *where Mr. Bredesen has been checked he has not spoken a human language,* but in two isolated instances where only one person was present, he spoke in a foreign language. Not knowing Mr. Bredesen, we shall take it for granted that he is sincere. Our judgment is that these two instances were cases where people misheard. They interpreted the sounds as a foreign language when in reality they were not.

If this was the work of the Holy Spirit, why was he left in denominationalism to preach some denominational doctrines? Bredesen tells us that he knows of Methodists, Baptists, Lutherans, Episcopalians, Presbyterians, and members of his own denomination (the Reformed Church of America) who have been baptized in the Spirit and have spoken with tongues. (*The Christian Reader,* p. 45) Bredesen is now minister of an independent church. If this is true, the Spirit has confirmed the conflicting doctrines of these denominations. How could the Spirit in the Bible confirm the word preached by the inspired men, who taught there is but one body and who taught against religious division, and also confirm the message of conflicting denominationalists today? (Mk. 16:17, 20; 1 Cor. 1:10-12; Eph. 4:1-6) Is the Spirit the author of contradictions? Pat Boone, for example, recognizes that baptism is immersion and that it is into Christ's body. (Acts 2:38; Rom. 6:2-5, 17-18; Gal. 3:26-27) And yet, he thinks these men whom he mentioned — at least some of whom differ with him on baptism and on the church — are miraculously guided, and their message miraculously confirmed, by the Holy Spirit. Pat will say he did not mean that everything they teach is right. However, if God is leading them in a supernatural way, why is He failing to lead them out of denominationalism? They are not being led by the Spirit as He speaks through the word, or they would abandon denominationalism. They are not being led by the same Spirit who inspired Paul, or they would abandon and oppose denominationalism. Without claiming to be a prophet — for such we are not — we predict that when Pat tries to lead these men, and many others who claim the miraculous baptism of the Spirit, to put on Christ in baptism, and teach this, he will find that most of them are not willing to let the Spirit lead them to do this. Perhaps someday Pat will wonder why. If so, will he give up the Pentecostal doctrines which he has embraced, or will he give up what the Spirit teaches on baptism, and on certain other subjects? Will his experiences lead him to change his mind about what the Bible teaches on such subjects?

OTHER CASES

R. A. Knox, in commenting on samples of tongues in the early part of the nineteenth century, wrote: "The philology of another world does not abide our question, but if we are to judge these results by merely human standards, we must admit that a child prattles no less convincingly." (*Enthusiasm,* p. 553)

Eugene A. Nida analyzed scores of tapes and tongues and concluded that they were not languages. (*Christianity Today,* Nov. 24, 1967, p. 40) Of course, tongues speakers may say that some of them are languages with which these linguists are unfamiliar. Since tongues are for a sign, why would the Spirit give them a language of a people to whom they cannot preach, and whose languages people in this country do not know? What would that be a sign of? Of what value is it to have a tongue and nobody to preach to who can hear in the language wherein they were born? (Acts 2:4, 6, 8, 11)

E. Mansell Pattison wrote that: "Investigation of the phenomenon has never verified the claim to speak in an actual foreign language unknown to the glossolalist. The glossolalist may use phonemes or fragments of a foreign language with which he may have had forgotten contact." ("Behavioral Science Research on the Nature of Glossolalia," *Journal of the American Scientific Affiliation,* Sept. 1968, p. 74)

Mormons have claimed tongues. One of their early apostles, Orson Pratt, said the gift was necessary in order to preach the gospel to foreigners (*Orson Pratt's Works,* Salt Lake City, Utah: George Cannon and Sons, 1891, pp. 99-100). However, Mormon missionaries have to learn the language of the people to whom they go. (*Millennial Star,* 1854, Vol. 16, p. 188, 190-191, 223, 236, 239, 254, 257, 365)

If an individual actually spoke in a language by some sort of supernatural gift, the author would still be obligated to test him by his teaching. Tongues in the New Testament were one of the signs which confirmed the word of God. (Mk. 16:17, 20) If tongues speakers confirm doctrines which are not in the Bible, or if they continue in religious organizations which teach false doctrine while claiming miraculous guidance of the Spirit, we know that they are not of God. In such a case, we would have to conclude that it was of the devil. Insofar as the author's own experience has gone, he has not known personally of any case which did not have a natural explanation.

RELIGION WITHOUT JOY

John L. Sherrill thought he might find some personal answers in his study of Pentecostalism. "Answers to the dryness in religious life that I felt and they apparently did not." After a time he concluded that they "had no answers, only fresh problems."

(*They Speak With Other Tongues,* p. 51) Later he concluded they had some answers.

Dullness and the lack of joy have led many individuals to seek for the solution in the tongues movement. In it there are many emotional experiences, as well as a sense of aliveness because they think they are inspired and miraculously gifted instruments of the Spirit. Some of them shy away from being labeled "inspired," but sooner or later they make claims and use expressions which indicate they are inspired at certain times. If they do not believe they are inspired, it is because they do not understand the nature of some of the gifts which they claim.

JOY IN CHRIST

Christians need to recognize there is joy in Christ. It is not identical with being on the mountain peaks of emotionalism at all times. It should come from our growing faith in God, from the conviction of victory if we continue to walk in the light, from the deep satisfactions which come from serving God and humanity, and from the blessed experience of giving rather than trying to be on the receiving end at all times. Too many grow up and take Christianity as a *part* of life along with a lot of other parts of life. Having never thought of what life would be like without Christ, failing to realize that Christ demands the whole of our lives, turning the following of Christ into a mere matter of assembling on certain days with others, and failing to live the life of service, it is no wonder that joy is lacking and dryness is present in such lives.

MIRACLES ESSENTIAL TO JOY?

It is assumed by some that there is no adequate basis, or at least insufficient motivation, for joy except through the baptism of the Spirit with miraculous manifestations. This is not sanctioned by the Spirit. However, those who think such is essential to joy, and who think they have received the Spirit in this way, rejoice. *A falsehood when believed has the same emotional impact on one which it would have if it were true.*

The seventy had two grounds for rejoicing which we do not have. *First,* they had the personal, physical presence of Jesus whom they could see and with whom they could talk face to face. (Lk. 10:1, 17) *Second,* they had miraculous power. "And the seventy returned with joy, saying, Lord, even the demons are subject unto us in thy name." Among other things Jesus said: "Behold, I have given you authority to tread upon serpents and scorpions, and over all the power of the enemy: and nothing shall in any wise hurt you." (Lk. 10:17, 19)

On the logic of some, we cannot have real joy as did they because no one claims that Christ is on earth today as He was then; and no one today actually has such power as is set forth in Lk. 10:19. If anyone says they do have this power we ask: in all honesty, does Lk. 10:19 describe you?

What did our Lord say? His statement to the seventy was not aimed at the logic of the ones with whom we are dealing, but it does demolish their logic. Although the seventy had such power, and the personal presence of Jesus, Jesus said: "Nevertheless *in this rejoice not, that the spirits are subject unto you; but rejoice that your names are written in heaven.*" (Lk. 10:20)

WITHOUT JOY?

In *Testimony* one of my friends tells us that before his baptism in the Holy Spirit, which included or resulted in tongues, he did not know much joy. He did have times of joy, but the great joy, he thinks, has come with the baptism in the Spirit and the miraculous gifts. How misguided he has been. How thoughtless of the great benefits which he had. He says he was saved, thus he believed his name was written in heaven, but still he did not have much joy. We have the hope of heaven, the cleansing by the blood of Jesus, the faith once for all delivered to the saints, the joy of fellowship in Christ, the joy of Bible study, the joy of service, the joy of love; but until we get the baptism of the Holy Spirit, and tongues, we can be a Christian for twenty-one years, as he was, and not really have the rejoicing which Christianity is supposed to bring to us. It is because we do not seek and get the baptism of the Holy Spirit!

There is something wrong when we find little joy, but the solution is not in the so-called baptism of the Spirit. Surely our Lord was not wrong when He said, even to those who had His personal presence and miraculous gifts, "nevertheless in this rejoice not, that the spirits are subject unto you; but rejoice that your names are written in heaven." (Lk. 10:20) Surely we have failed to follow Jesus' way of joy, and not through a failure to be baptized miraculously in the Spirit, when we do not find our great joy in our names being written in heaven. Surely we have failed to meditate sufficiently on what it means to have this living hope of the incorruptible, undefiled, non-fading eternal inheritance which is reserved in heaven for us, and which we cannot miss as long as we allow God to guard us through faith. (1 Pet. 1:3-5)

One cannot miss it if he follows Peter's prescription as to how can "be richly supplied unto you the entrance into the eternal kingdom of our Lord and Saviour Jesus Christ." (2 Pet. 1:2-11) A sense of joy does not guarantee our eternal salvation, but the assurance of eternal salvation should generate joy. We do not know we are saved because we rejoice, but we rejoice because we know we are saved.

Our name is written in the Lamb's book of life when we obey the gospel, and become sons of God through the new birth. (John 3:3-5; Matt. 28:19; Acts 2:38; 22:16; Rom. 6:2-5, 17-18; Gal. 3:26-27; Phil. 4:3) We must be faithful unto death so that our names will not be taken out of the book of life. (Rev. 3:5; 13:8; 2:12, 15; 21:27; 22:19)

HOW KNOW?

There are those, however, who say that they cannot know their names are in the Lamb's book of life unless they have the baptism of the Spirit with miraculous manifestations. There is no passage of scripture which says that such must come to each individual so he can have the assurance of salvation. Miracles were involved in the revelation and confirmation of the gospel (Heb. 2:3-4), but not everyone received miraculous manifestations. Some who depend on miracles for their assurance will be disappointed on Judgment day. (Matt. 7:21-23) Although there were many gifts in Corinth, this did not prove it was a truly spiritual congregation. At least some of them stood in danger of falling, and all needed to take heed. (1 Cor. 1:10-13; 2:1ff; 10:1ff, etc.) Our assurance is based on the word of God. The people in Samaria were forgiven, and knew they were forgiven, before the apostles laid hands on any of them. (Acts 8:12-18) How do we know we are saved? Because God said so, if we have been baptized into the death, burial, and resurrection of Christ and walk in the newness of life. (Acts 2:38; Rom. 6:2-5, 17-18) Is not God's word good enough for us? How could the Spirit speak plainer? He speaks through the written Word. The failure to believe God has forgiven us is a failure to trust what God has said. He will do what He has promised when we do what He has commanded. (Matt. 28:19; Mk. 16:15-16; Acts 2:38; Rom. 4:20-21) To ask for miraculous confirmation of one's forgiveness, and to prove that one's name is written in heaven, is to say, in effect whether one realizes it or not, that God's word is not good enough for us. We must have something more.

Perhaps someone may say that he trusts God's word but he cannot trust himself to know whether he has obeyed God's gospel.

If you can't how can you trust yourself to know whether you must have the baptism of the Spirit, how to seek it, and to know that you have found it? God no more does your knowing for you than He does your hearing, believing, and obeying for you. *The Holy Spirit through Paul said that the spirit of man can know the things of man.* You can know whether you have obeyed the gospel from the heart, and you can, therefore, know whether God has forgiven you. But you can know what the gospel is, and how to obey it, only through the study of the word of God. For therein is revealed the mind of God through the men inspired by the Holy Spirit. (1 Cor. 2:10-13) When our spirit bears witness that we have done what the Spirit says we must do to become a child of God, and that we are doing what the Spirit says we must do to remain a child of God, the Spirit bears witness with (this is a co-witnessing) our spirit that we are children of God. (Rom. 8:16) The author has discussed this in some detail in *The Holy Spirit and the Christian.*

Instead of seeking the baptism of the Spirit with miraculous manifestations, search the scriptures daily to find out what you must do to become, and to remain, a Christian, and then do it in faith trusting in His Word. Being thus assured by the Spirit through the word of God, you can rejoice that your name is written in heaven.

RESISTING THE SPIRIT?

It is possible for religious people to resist the Spirit. Stephen said: "Ye stiffnecked and uncircumcised in heart and ears, ye do always resist the Holy Spirit: as your fathers did, so do ye. Which of the prophets did not your fathers persecute? and they killed them that showed before of the coming of the Righteous One; of whom ye have now become betrayers and murderers; ye who received the law as it was ordained by angels, and kept it not". (Acts 7:51-53) Why was resistance to the prophets resistance to the Spirit? Because the prophets spoke by the Spirit. "Yet many years didst thou bear with them, and testifiedst against them *by thy Spirit through thy prophets:* yet would they not give ear: therefore gavest thou them into the hand of the peoples of the lands. Nevertheless in thy manifold mercies thou didst not make a full end of them, nor forsake them; for thou art a gracious and meriful God". (Neh. 9:30-31) To refuse to accept and follow the message of the Spirit was to resist the Spirit.

There are those who maintain that in rejecting the position that the miraculous gifts are for us today, and in opposing those who claim these gifts, we are resisting the Spirit. We are obligated to resist claims of men to be prophets of God unless they produce the necessary proof. We must repudiate those who claim to be apostles, for example, but are not. (Rev. 2:2) We need to prove all things, and hold fast that which is good for there are false prophets who claim to work miracles. (Matt. 7:21-23; 1 Thess. 5:21; 2 Thess. 2:10-12; 1 John 4:1-2) Basically, we must make two tests. *First,* do they do the mighty works that a prophet of God could do? How do their accomplishments look in the light of their claim and of the Bible? *Second,* we must test them by their teaching. Regardless of what they do, if they lead us contrary to the New Testament we must reject them. So far as my own experience and reading has revealed, these people do not do the wide variety of signs and wonders in the Bible, and sooner or later they contradict the Bible.

TRAGEDIES PROOF OF RESISTING THE SPIRIT?

One person who claims the gift of tongues, but does not claim to be a prophet, said that he is troubled and deeply saddened that, in contrast to what his family is experiencing, there are many who have judged him harshly and said he was deluded who have suffered terrible tragedies in their own lives, their children, and their work. "More and more I feel that this is the result of resisting the Holy Spirit and His urgent pleading with the children of God today to avail themselves of the power needed to resist this last vicious onslaught of the devil and his angels. I don't see it as the punishment of God — but rather the unchecked harassment of the thief, the killer and the destroyer of our souls. . . . Because we so often deny the supernatural power of God available to Christians now, we become subject to the supernatural onslaughts and vicious attacks of satan."

If the Bible teaches that these gifts are for us today, and if they have the gifts and we oppose them, we are resisting the Spirit. If these people are right, there should be apostles and prophets also today and we would be resisting the Spirit in resisting their message and this would include their written message — which would be scripture.

Concerning the position of this friend, we observe. *First,* we appreciate his compassion and concern. *Second,* those who think he is deluded are viewed by him as resisting the Spirit. *Third,* those who have been harsh with him have failed to follow the teaching of the Spirit in this matter. Of course, sometimes we may think a person is harsh because he has had to take a plain stand against something we believe. *Fourth,* there are those who have been right in certain teachings and wrong in their attitudes and manner of life. They may reap the consequences of these things in their own lives and these things may have a bad influence on their families. This is a judgment of God through His law of sowing and reaping. He brings evil on us, the fruit of our own thought. (Jer. 6:19; Gal. 6:7-8) *Fifth,* we must be careful about judging the quality of a life by the tragedies which have entered that life. The Galileans whom Pilate killed, and those on whom the tower in Siloam fell, were not sinners above the rest of the men because they suffered these things. (Luke 13:1-5) Paul suffered numerous tragedies, far above the other apostles, but this did not prove that he was resisting the Spirit. (2 Cor. 11:23-33) He also had a thorn in the flesh. It was a messenger of satan, even though Paul had supernatural power. (2 Cor. 12:7-10) Although I do not know exactly when it is being done, and although I do not identify it with those things which come to both saints and sinners alike, I know that there is a chastening which cometh from the Lord and which is an indication of sonship. (Heb. 12:4-13)

There are things which happen to us from which we can learn much. It may be they call our attention to some neglect, or to something which we have done which was wrong. We should always ask how we can learn and profit by these experiences. However, they are not the test as to whether we are walking in the will of God. The only test of this is found in the revealed will of God. Although there are things which happen in our lives which reveal wherein we have failed, it is not through the tragedies of our lives but through the truth that we know our standing before God.